Stay Wild,

Heather

transform the shoulds into coulds, or cans, or even simple no's."
—RACHEL SUMAN, chief experience officer,
International Association of Administrative
Professionals (IAAP)

"*Grounded Wildness* is transformative and inspirational! Anyone seeking advice on how to live a more authentic life should read this book. *Grounded Wildness* will guide you to seek out joy, trust yourself, and unapologetically take up space. It will show you how to become the whole version of yourself again. It has been a motivating and enlightening experience to read this book!"
—TONESHIA ADDISON, Tennessee Banker's Women
in Banking 2023 conference chair

"This book is a must-read for every woman swimming in perfectionism, pleasing, and performing, and who is looking for the permission to be her wildest, most beautiful self."
—SHARON PODOBNIK, founder of
The Center for Conscious Leadership
and author of *It's Not (All) Your Fault*

"*Grounded Wildness* is a roadmap for women who are ready to ditch the suffocating rules that have kept them small—and can't wait to reclaim their freedom."
—GABY NATALE, Triple Daytime EMMY-winning
journalist, speaker, and bestselling author

Grounded

Wildness

Grounded
Wildness

Break Free from Performing Your Life and Start Living It

Heather Whelpley

Minneapolis, MN

ISBN 13: 978-1-63489-659-7

Library of Congress Catalog Number has been applied for.

Printed in the United States of America

First Printing: 2023

27   26   25   24   23   5   4   3   2   1

Cover design by Jess Morphew

Interior design by Zoe Norvell

Wise Ink Creative Publishing
807 Broadway St. NE
Suite 46
Minneapolis, MN 55413

For you
And for me

TABLE OF CONTENTS

PART FOUR: Getting Grounded and Wild

Introduction

It's my favorite picture ever taken of me. I'm eight years old. It's 1988, and I *look* 1988. I'm wearing a head-to-toe pastel pink sweatsuit adorned with a large red satin heart across the chest. My naturally stick-straight brown hair is growing out a perm, creating uneven waves across my bangs and shoulder-length locks. My mom had recently decided I would be more comfortable if I didn't have to tuck my hair behind my ears to keep it from getting in my face, so the sides of my growing-out perm are shaved off and I'm sporting a *mullet*.

I'm looking directly at the camera, my blue eyes shining at the lens. I have a calm yet slightly audacious smile on my face. My arm is stretched out to the camera, and I'm holding a *live snake*.

This is no minuscule garter snake! Its camouflage-checked body winds through the air three or four feet in front of me. My right hand grips the snake lightly, just below its head, while its tail wraps around my left hand as an anchor.

I look at this little girl and see someone who knows exactly who she is. She's confident, bold, and relaxed. There's no distance between who she is on the inside and the person she's presenting to the world. She has nothing to hide, cover up, or shove down. She's taking up the full space of who she is.

This little girl *is* me. I'm the girl, now a woman, who looks straight at the camera with a smile on her face while holding a live snake. That's me.

I lost her for a long time.

Maybe lost is too strong of a word. It's more like she got buried under an avalanche of rules that told me to hold my breath and tuck myself in.

These rules commanded me to quiet the boldness of my voice and dampen the fire in my belly. They made it clear that I should be ashamed of the larger body I inhabited throughout my teen and young adult years. They guided me to shove down the big emotions I felt, put a smile on my face, and keep going. They ordered me to prove my worth through productivity, achievement, likability, and a million other forms of external validation.

Then I woke up.

I started to break the rules.

That journey began with severing the ties between my worth and achievement. My first book, *An Overachiever's*

Guide to Breaking the Rules: How to Let Go of Perfect and Live Your Truth, details the story of this initial awakening. For the first time, I saw clearly all the messages, stories, and rules I'd been handed that had told me I *always* had to work harder and do more—and I realized I could choose to let go of those rules.

These realizations were HUGE. It's not an exaggeration to say they changed my life.

Little did I know, that was just the beginning. Another level of realizations and rule-breaking was on the horizon and about to split open my entire world.

I was about to become a woman living in *grounded wildness*.

Grounded wildness is the wholeness you rediscover when you break the rules that have broken you—and the inevitable freedom that follows. You stand wild in your freedom because you are grounded in your worth. You get to stop *performing* your life and start *living* it.

My journey into grounded wildness has been a pilgrimage to break away from the suffocating rules that kept me small and tight and to reclaim my freedom. It's a kind of freedom that doesn't require achievement, validation, or compliance, but rather lives deep inside me. Inside all of us.

This freedom allows me to feel every emotion I'm experiencing, from the joy of laughing with total abandon to an overflowing river of grief. It lets me get on stage and say the thing that needs to be said, rather than worrying if I'm pushing too hard or upsetting the status quo too much. It lets me go on a date without feeling like I have to perform and prove that I'm fun and desirable. It allows me to be my own guide, rather than looking toward the rules to tell me how I should look, speak, show up, and generally live my life.

Grounded wildness has opened the door for the little girl holding the snake to come back to life. Only now, that little girl has grown up. She's a truer version of herself because she's broken through the rules handed to her and made up her own rules for life. She knows she is whole, complete, and even *radiant* without having to do anything at all. No proving, pleasing, or perfecting needed.

I want this for you as well.

Parts of this book will make you feel happy and light. Other parts will make you uncomfortable. You'll recognize the rules that have kept you performing and be reminded of your own wildness. You might cry. You'll probably laugh. Questions will arise. You'll have new realizations.

I encourage you to stay awake for it all. To feel everything you're feeling without judgment. When something gets uncomfortable, sit with the discomfort and listen for the messages it's sending you. When something gives you joy, grant yourself full permission to wrap yourself in that joy and feel it in your soul. This is all part of living in grounded wildness.*

---

* If it ever feels like too much, seek out a therapist, counselor, or other professional. This book wouldn't have been possible without the therapist I worked with for six months. She guided me through the breakdown that led to grounded wildness. You'll read more about this experience in part two, The Break.

This book is broken into four parts. The first three detail my journey from losing my young wildness through many years of relentless performing, and finally to the breaks that led me to escape the rules, rediscover myself, and move into the freedom of grounded wildness. As you read my story, you'll be prompted to reflect on your journey. I invite you to spend time on these exercises. This book isn't about me. It's about you. Only you can uncover your story and reclaim your freedom.

The fourth and final part is called "Getting Grounded and Wild." It outlines practices to guide you toward grounded wildness—and stay there. You'll learn how to create space for yourself, feel your feelings, follow your aliveness, trust your knowing, let your body lead, claim yourself, and take up space. You'll also discover how to deal with the people who don't get it (or who straight-up disapprove) and find your grounded wildness community of people who *do*.

Even though I present practices for you to try, this isn't a precise how-to book—and that's on purpose. I can't tell you exactly how grounded wildness looks and feels for you. I can't give you a ten-point process to check off that will guarantee your "success." You can't hack your way into your own freedom.

Your path to grounded wildness is a continual journey. I regularly discover new rules I had no idea were living inside me. Old ones also occasionally pop up and require me to slow down, reconnect to myself, and consciously let them go again.

And yet, I'm experiencing a freedom I didn't know was possible a few years ago. I feel that freedom coursing through my veins, enlivening my body, heart, mind, and soul. I've stopped hiding in the shadows of myself and stepped into the light.

You can too.

Let's get started.

—Part One—

The Years of Performing

CHAPTER 1

From Wildness to Performing

I lost my wildness in seventh grade.

There had been a few hits to my wildness before middle school (I have diary entries tracking my Weight-Watchers points at ten years old). But up until seventh grade, I was the girl smiling at the camera and holding the snake about 95 percent of the time.

In sixth grade, a few months before the rules began to crush my wildness, I went with my class to Wolf Ridge Environmental Learning Center in northern Minnesota. During our five days at camp, we hiked, learned survival skills in the snow, dissected owl pellets, and howled at the nearby wolves—and they howled back! I loved every second.

One evening, at our nightly bonfire, a counselor asked us to arrange ourselves on a continuum, from "I don't care at all what people think, and I do my own thing" to "I care a lot about what other people think." Most of my classmates spread out somewhere along the middle. I, on the other hand, lodged myself squarely on the furthest side of the line, signifying "I don't care what people think."

The same counselor who'd asked us to line up looked at me with a smile and said, "I thought you'd be there."

That was me. The twelve-year-old who knew herself so well, she didn't need to care about what other people thought of her.

It didn't last long.

In seventh grade, I moved from my tiny alternative elementary school—where we did entirely self-paced learning and had no desks, no names on the board, and no actual rules that I remember—to a neighboring traditional middle school, where we all sat in desks, did the same lessons, and definitely had rules. This was a good school, academically speaking. I had great friends, many of whom I'm still friends with today. I wasn't ever bullied. In the realm of how this transition could have gone, it was better than what nearly every other middle schooler would have experienced in a similar situation.

Even so, this was the moment when I started to perform. I sprinted from my secure spot of "I don't care what people think" to about three-quarters down the line toward

"I care a lot about what other people think" and took up residence there.

In sixth grade, my favorite outfit was a bright green shirt and matching pants with a rainbow belt tied around my waist, accompanied by shoulder-length silver salamander earrings and a pair of Keds covered in flowers. None of this was "in." I didn't care.

In seventh grade, I asked for Girbaud jeans for Christmas, THE brand of 1992. They were boring and uncomfortable. I wanted them anyway.

In sixth grade, I painted giant, colorful flowers on poster boards. I didn't worry about how they looked or if they were "good." I just loved the act of putting paint to paper.

In seventh grade, I cowered away from art, suddenly aware that my drawings and paintings didn't look how they were "supposed to" look.

In sixth grade, I was curious and creative; and I put myself out there in every sense of the word. I *wanted* to stand out. I wanted to be fully me.

In seventh grade, I started to hide my full self. I wondered if all of me was just a little bit too much. I felt like I needed to follow the rules to fit in.

In sixth grade, I was me.

In seventh grade, I started to perform.

It's not a surprise I gained thirty pounds in the first semester of seventh grade. I got bigger on the outside as I squished myself down on the inside. I unknowingly craved a return to my full, bold, whole self; and I tried in vain to satisfy that hunger with food. Binging became my release for holding it all in. It was a coping mechanism that stayed with me for over a decade.

Gaining weight had its consequences, particularly given that I came of age in an era that glorified heroin chic as the ultimate standard of beauty. Shame was an immediate byproduct. Within a few years, I overemphasized achievement to compensate for that shame. The proving, pleasing, and perfecting that resulted started in school and continued into the workplace, dating, and my life as a whole.

When I entered my first corporate job in my late twenties, I continued those patterns of performing—and added a new layer. Unlike my sprint down the line to "I care what people think" in seventh grade, this new layer happened at a snail's pace over several years. This is the deepest and scariest walk away from yourself, because it happens so slowly that you don't even notice the change. You become normalized to the version of you that is performing—so much so that the performing you feels like the *real* you. The rules you're following become so indoctrinated, you don't realize their power over you. And you think, *This is just the way it is.*

This was my ten-year foray into full-time employment in corporate America. When I started working at a large company in grad school, the overachiever in me wanted to do everything well—which led to me saying yes too often, trying to do everything on my own, and generally overworking.

At the beginning, though, I didn't hold my voice back. I cared nothing about hierarchy and corporate org charts. I respected leaders as people, but their titles didn't scare me at all—even the big titles with a C at the front. I had no problem offering up my opinion, from disagreeing with my direct manager to sharing my thoughts openly with senior leaders. I remember going to a colleague's baby shower a few years after this first job, and my since-retired department head telling me I hadn't been afraid to put her or other senior leaders "in their place."

She meant it as a compliment.

Over the years, though, corporate culture quieted that strong voice. It tucked my wildness further inside of me and told me to hush. It was in the feedback I got that said I could be too direct, then too accommodating, and then too direct again. It was in my discovery that I needed to ask for permission and gain approval before taking action. It was in my being told that I couldn't disagree with my manager in front of other people, only behind closed doors.

Let me be clear: None of my colleagues would have described me as "quiet." I still asked big questions. I still voiced my opinion. But I learned to do so cautiously. Not thoughtfully, but cautiously. It became a carefully curated performance to avoid judgment. Another step away from my innate wildness.

Don't worry. This will all fall apart soon.

CHAPTER 2

The Ways You Perform

Performing is anything that takes YOU away from YOU. It's the front you put on that covers up your true desires and emotions. It's the armor you use to protect yourself from the judgment, criticism, and sideways glances that indicate you've broken some unwritten rule about how you're *supposed* to show up. It's the words, actions, and decisions that feel just a little bit off, even if you can't quite put your finger on why.

Performing generally comes down to four overlapping categories: proving, pleasing, perfecting, and rebelling. Yes, rebelling. I know that word sticks out in this group like one of those standardized test questions where you have to choose the item that doesn't fit the pattern. Rebelling, though, is as much of a performance trap as proving, pleasing, or perfecting. I'll share more about why later in the chapter.

Let's dive into each type of performing in more detail.

Proving

This was me. I certainly had pleasing, perfecting, and a little rebelling thrown into my performing, but proving took up the most amount of energy and space in my life. So much so that the very first chapter of *An Overachiever's Guide to Breaking the Rules* is called, "What Are You <u>Proving</u>?"

My proving showed up most obviously in school and work, at least in the outward sense. Although I didn't always follow a traditional path or feel like I had to check a bunch of boxes to show I was successful, I constantly proved myself through overdoing and achievement.

In my younger years, I was at the top of my high school class, was captain of two sports, worked at my church, and volunteered—all at the same time. In my corporate career, I always raised my hand for the next project, executed everything on my already overflowing plate, and rarely set boundaries. As an entrepreneur, I felt like everything I launched had to be successful, I had to match my corporate salary right away, and I had to prove I could hack it on my own.[*]

All these forms of proving and my journey to let them go are detailed in *An Overachiever's Guide to Breaking the Rules*. There's another category, however, that I only touched on in that book. I mentioned it in the first chapter of *An Overachiever's Guide* as the root of my proving, then jumped right back into overachieving for the rest of the book.

In short, I was proving my desirability to men.

This proving was buried way beneath the overachiever, under layers of shame that kept me bolted within myself, locked into a protective shield that kept part of me hidden for decades. During this time, I fought to show I was desirable because I didn't believe it could be true. Every single message the world had sent me during my childhood and teen years had told me that my larger body was ugly, disgusting, and something to be ashamed of. Those messages declared that no man could ever want my body. How could they want such a disgusting, shameful thing?

Instead of seeing the errors and lies in the messages I'd received, I believed something was wrong with *me*. It was *my* fault I couldn't control myself around food. *My* fault I couldn't exercise off all the calories I consumed. *My* fault I couldn't be the pretty size 2 that was the standard of desire.

Clearly, I was broken.

When you believe you're broken, you do a whole lot of performing to try and compensate. To prove you're worthy in spite

---

[*]   For the record, that did NOT happen. I failed often, and it took three to four years to match my corporate salary.

of the brokenness. To put on the appearance of wholeness regardless of the shattered pieces of glass you feel stabbing at your insides. To smile and pretend everything is fine, good, or even *great* while you secretly wonder how in God's name you will ever fix everything that's wrong with you and finally become lovable, enough, worthy, and (in my case) desirable.

How do you become whole when you believe a part of you is broken beyond repair?

I attempted this for years. I didn't believe men could be physically attracted to me, so I worked to prove I was MORE than enough in every other area of my life. I strived to show the men I was interested in that I was smart, fun, adventurous, creative, and everything they really wanted if they could just get to know the *real* me. I proved through every comment, every laugh, and every social media post I thought they would like. I proved by listening to the podcasts and bands they recommended, reading the books and poetry they enjoyed, and attempting to show everything we had in common as if that would convince them we were destined to be together. I never did things I actively disagreed with or were against my values. But I definitely performed, like a little marionette on stage, desperately longing to be noticed.

I believed if I could somehow prove myself to men in all these other categories, then the desirability wouldn't matter. If all the other pieces of the pie were overflowing, wouldn't that make up for my broken body?

In practical terms, the answer was no. I dated men before coming into my grounded wildness, but only a few made it past the third date—and most of those dates weren't all that fun to begin with. For the better part of my adulthood, I shied away from sex and anything physical, first because I was ashamed of my body and later because I was ashamed of my lack of sexual experience. I had a lot of male friends (several of whom I had crushes on throughout the years), but they never saw me as anything more than a friend. I felt visible as a person, but invisible as a woman.

None of this gets to the heart of the matter, though: that I was never broken at all. Of course, I didn't know this when I was mired in shame and drowning in proving. It took breaking away from the rules to understand—and finally free myself.

This is the core of my proving story. Your proving might be completely different from mine. To better understand your proving, think of it this way: Anything you do to demonstrate your worth is proving. It can show up in rules like these:

- I'm not the smartest in the room, so I have to work the hardest.
- I have to be productive all the time.
- I have to do it all—and do it all well.
- I have to keep it all together all the time.
- I have to do it all myself. I don't need any help.
- I have to be busy, get the highest ranking on my performance review or the best grades, or say yes to everything to demonstrate I'm valuable.
- I have to show them I deserve to be their friend, partner, daughter, parent, etc.
- If I achieve, have the right house, the right job, the right body, and/or say the right thing, then people

will like me.

Pleasing

Proving may have been the core of my performing, but pleasing was threaded through the proving like a matrix, little wisps of yarn pulling the proving together tight.

For example, I grew up active—*very* active—in a Lutheran church in Minnesota. My first job was working in children's ministries at this church when I was just fourteen. I was involved with the youth group throughout middle school and high school. I even interned for two summers at this church when I was in college.

I have immeasurable gratitude for my experiences at this church—along with a few things that needed to be unlearned, but mostly gratitude. As a Sunday school leader, I learned how to be on stage and command an audience at a young age by storytelling and singing silly songs in front of hundreds of kids. My church youth group was the one place I could be myself when I felt confused and stuck between other groups of friends in high school. I learned that adults can be silly, playful, and responsible all at once through working with our amazing children's ministries director. I wouldn't be the person I am today without these experiences.

As I sauntered into my twenties, though, traditional church didn't feel right anymore. I stopped going, but at the same time, I worried about what all these people who supported me for so long would think. Would they be disappointed that I was no longer a fully believing, active Christian?

Pleasing showed up in my work experience as well. In my thirties, my job changed in a way that was outside of my control—and in a way I hated. I knew something in my career would need to change, but I didn't know what. So as I figured out my next steps, I continued to do this job I despised.

I was working on a great team, but whenever I sat in meetings with them, my entire body SCREAMED at me to get up and RUN out of the room. I twitched below the surface, wanting to yell out all the feelings I had shoved down. I longed to leave it all behind and figure out the details later.

No one had a clue.

I was a master at putting on a happy face and saying the things people wanted to hear. I was aware of my emotions and my body's reactions, but I clenched them down so effectively that no one could sense I was anything but completely content and happy in my new job. It was the ultimate pleasing performance.

Eventually, I left that job to start my business and began to speak professionally on topics like imposter syndrome and creating your own rules for success. I wanted to challenge systems, structures, and bias in my presentations, but I worried about pushing the status quo too hard, particularly when it came to talking about discrimination. My inner voice, however, told me to be *more* direct about discrimination. My knowing said to lay it out on the table and tell the truth about how patriarchy and white supremacy played a role in imposter syndrome and held people back from sharing their authentic voices with the world. My values and intuition urged me to talk about the tightrope people from underrepresented groups walk every day to avoid judgment and criticism.

Instead of speaking directly, though, I pleased by skirting around the issues. When I spoke about the reasons people experience imposter syndrome, I had a slide that listed power structures as a core reason why underrepresented groups tend to experience the impacts of imposter syndrome more strongly than white, straight, cisgender men. The words *discrimination*, *racism*, *bias*, and *microaggressions* were absent from my presentation, however. I held back my voice and kept pleasing both to maintain my own comfort and to avoid making those who benefit from patriarchy and white supremacy uncomfortable.[*]

There's one more manner of pleasing that impacts so many women that I want to call it out directly: feeling like you shouldn't be "too much." I hear it all the time—and I've felt it myself.

One of my former coaching clients only wore black because she felt like dressing in bold colors would push people over the edge in her "too much-ness." She held back on how she wanted to dress because, somewhere along the line, she'd gotten the message that she needed to mute herself to appease others.

Similarly, I was dating a man after I came into

---

[*] This has since been rectified. I now have a slide that directly lists bias, discrimination, and microaggressions as core reasons for why many people experience imposter syndrome.

my grounded wildness, and it came up in conversation that I hardly drink any caffeine. When I told him this, he looked at me and said, "Yeah . . . I don't think you need any caffeine."

He wasn't smiling when he said it. There was no jovial affection in his tone.

A little pit dropped into my stomach. I was simultaneously angry, hurt, and a touch ashamed. He didn't love, appreciate, or even accept my big energy. Instead, I got the feeling he wanted to quiet it down.

Part of me wanted to give him a big, "Screw you. If you can't handle ALL of me, then you can walk right out the door." In that moment, though, I smiled and carried on the conversation, the little pit of worrying if I was too much for him still residing in my belly.*

Perhaps these stories are reminding you of your examples. Pleasing also shows up in the rules we're taught that lead to these stories, including the following:

- I can't disappoint anyone.
- I should just nod and go along.
- It's my job to take care of everyone.
- I can't say no.
- I shouldn't burden anyone.
- I have to be nice and polite.
- Good girls don't get angry.
- It's selfish to do what I want.
- I have to keep everyone happy.

---

*   We're not dating anymore.

Perfecting

I never considered myself a perfectionist. Overachiever? Yes. Overdoer? Absolutely. Perfectionist? Not so much.

I viewed a perfectionist as someone who spent hours reviewing emails and PowerPoint decks to make sure there were no typos and confirm (multiple times) that everything looked completely perfect.

This was never me. I've always believed we're all human—and humans make errors. We miss things. That's just the way it is. I believe this so deeply that I would get annoyed whenever someone seemed upset by a minor error I'd made or whenever I saw someone spend copious amounts of time to make something inconsequential look so pretty it could have been in a Martha Stewart catalog. I thought that level of perfection was a complete waste of time.

Then I learned the *real* definition of perfectionism: holding yourself (and sometimes others) to unrealistically high standards—and then criticizing yourself when you don't meet those standards.

I wasn't a perfectionist when it came to the details, but I was *definitely* a perfectionist when it came to the big things. I expected myself to make the right decisions all the time, remember everything I'd ever learned, give absolutely fantastic answers in every Q&A in every speaking engagement, and succeed at everything in my career the first time I did it.

And I thought I wasn't a perfectionist. Ha!

To be fair, proving was at the root of many of these perfectionist behaviors. All of the three *P*s overlap in an attempt to mitigate shame brought on by the rules of how you are "supposed to" be.

Here are some additional perfecting rules you might feel:

- It has to be perfect before I can share it.
- I *always* have to do my best, regardless of whether the situation requires my best.
- I'm not allowed to fail—or even make mistakes.
- I have to make the right decisions all the time.
- I can't let anyone see my mess.
- I have to look pretty, be the "right" weight, have a clean and beautiful home, have the right job, etc., etc., etc.

Do you see yourself in this list? Or in the ones for proving and pleasing?

Proving, pleasing, and perfecting all have one thing in common: conforming. When you perform through proving, pleasing, and/or perfecting, you are molding yourself to fit the standards passed along to you. You are wearing a beautifully painted shield of armor that separates the full you from the parts you show to the world. Meanwhile, your wild and grounded self is banging against the inside of that armor, screaming with all her might, "Just let me free!"

This is proving, pleasing, and perfecting. It's conforming.

Rebelling is the other side of the same coin. It's completely different, yet exactly the same.

Rebelling

Rebelling often looks like freedom. It shows up like a giant middle finger to the rules you've been taught. It frequently resembles an independent woman making her way in the world regardless of what anyone else thinks.

Sometimes what we perceive as rebelling really is freedom. And sometimes it's as much of a performance trap as proving, pleasing, and perfecting.

How can you tell the difference? It's all in the energy.

Rebelling is going against yourself to do something different just because it's different. It's acting in opposition to your values simply to push against what you've been taught. It's breaking the rules *on* purpose, but not *with* purpose.

When proving, pleasing, and perfecting, you're *conforming to*. But when rebelling, you're *pushing against*. Neither one is freedom. Neither one is grounded wildness. Neither one is you.

In my experience, performing through proving, pleasing, and perfecting is more common than performing through rebelling. But I do see it—in other people and, occasionally, in myself. Rebelling wasn't common for me (looking back, I think it would have been helpful for me to rebel and push boundaries more when I was younger!). But when it did show up, it was often around food and alcohol.

When I was younger, I found a freedom in binging that I didn't feel in the rest of my life. Even after I lost weight, binging still found me. It was both a rebellion against the rules I'd been taught and a respite from the proving, pleasing, and perfecting I was doing in my life. Alcohol occasionally served the same function. I let down my proving armor when I had a few (or more) cocktails and found a similar abandon to eating an entire loaf of bread or downing a pint of ice cream. I felt the temporary freedom of losing control, but *I* wasn't free.

Rebelling may show up for you like this:

- Dating someone who feels like the freedom you desire, even though you know they aren't a healthy force in your life.
- Downing a bottle of wine on a Tuesday evening. Or any evening. Because you can.
- Staying single and being the picture of a strong, independent woman because the world isn't going to dictate to you that women should be in a relationship, even though you'd love to be in a great partnership.
- Bungee jumping because all the men in your group have done it and none of the women have—and my God, you're not going to let that happen, even if you are terrified (and not in a good way) and have no actual desire to jump off the platform and fall toward the river like a rag doll.
- Refusing to listen to feedback because no one else gets to dictate anything about you to you.
- Rejecting the latest trend—whether that's clothing, a kitchen appliance, or a best-selling book—because everyone else is doing it, even though you like the trendy clothes, would use the kitchen appliance all the time, or have a feeling you'd love the book.
- Showing up ready to fight in your work meetings because you are a force to be reckoned with and *someone* needs to be pushing back, even if you sometimes agree with the decisions being made.
- Avoiding implementing traditional systems in your business because you shun how other entrepreneurs

operate, even though some of those systems will save you time, make things more efficient, and give you *more* freedom.*

- Refusing to be the one who cooks in your marriage because that's the traditional patriarchal role of a wife and you are NOT going to fulfill that role, regardless of what would work for you and your relationship.

Rebelling isn't you in the same way proving, pleasing, and perfecting aren't you. They may be different ways of performing, but they're the same trap.

Why You Perform

There's one overarching message I want you to take away from this section: *Performing is not your fault*.

Performing comes from the rules you've been taught about what it means to be a good girl, woman, parent, employee, and leader, as well as a productive, contributing member of society. You did not make up these rules. They come from the messages you've received every day, from the time you were born until right now.

The strongest rules often come from your family.

---

*　　I recently realized I was rebelling in this exact way—and I didn't even know I was doing it! I discovered my desire to run my business 100 percent according to my own rules resulted in some stubbornness in listening to what works for others and considering that (shocker of all shockers) some of it may work for me too.

They're buried so deep in your schema that you don't even realize they're operating in the background of your day-to-day decisions. The people around you earliest in your life told you directly and indirectly what was acceptable (and not acceptable) through their words, actions, and what you were praised and punished for. You learned what was respectable and what was shameful by what was critiqued, admired, openly discussed, shoved down, or simply not talked about.

When I do a speaking engagement that incorporates these rules, the deepest realizations from audience members are often about the family rules they didn't know they were following until the moment I mention a rule—and they are suddenly flooded with the overwhelming recognition that it's controlling aspects of their life. These are some things that have come up:

- I was always told I was the pillar of my family and that I set the example for all my brothers and sisters. Twenty years later, I still feel like I have to be the example for them!
- My parents expected me to become a doctor, lawyer, or engineer. I feel like I disappointed them by choosing a different path—and like I have to make up for that disappointment in other ways.
- Feelings weren't talked about in my family. I learned to smile and pretend everything was fine, no matter how I felt.

Your family isn't the only source of your rules, however. They can originate from your school days, when you were likely rewarded for sitting quietly at your desk, doing what you were told, and literally and figuratively coloring inside the lines. They have also trickled in through every source of media, from *Seventeen* magazine to MTV to LinkedIn. If you're my age, those media messages told you that petite and thin was the desired body type when you were in high school, then catapulted you into adulthood by expecting you to be a superwoman capable of holding your work, parenting, marriage, social life, and community involvement together all the time—and being successful at all of it.

Every perfectionistic and productivity-obsessed work culture you've been a part of engrained these rules on a deeper level. Every toxic boss that shamed you for making a mistake, threw you daggers (or worse) when you spoke up in a meeting with leaders, or required eight people to review your PowerPoint deck before it was presented reinforced the rules you were taught.

Some of these rules are passed down to nearly everyone, at least in the United States. Hustle culture is being challenged, but it still currently reigns as the desired norm. Employees are often expected to go above and beyond to the point of sacrificing their well-being so that they can be seen as having high potential and deserving of promotions, raises, and development opportunities. Individuals can set boundaries, but when those boundaries are constantly pushed, it's hard to maintain them over time—especially if you've also been handed rules that tie your worth to productivity and achievement.

Many of the rules I've talked about in this book, however,

are rooted in discrimination. They are the expectations taught to those who were viewed by the world as girls when they were young and women as adults. They are the box of what is considered to be a good, successful, likable female.

These rules don't impact all women equally, either. Women of color may feel greater pressure to prove, please, and perfect because they are judged more harshly than white women when they make a mistake, show emotion, or take any steps outside the box of acceptability. Many black women in particular have shared that they were told their entire lives, "You have to be twice as good, and you're not allowed to make any mistakes." I was never handed that rule.

Let me say it again: *These rules are not your fault.* PLEASE do not feel shame, guilt, judgment, or embarrassment for performing in accordance with them. If any of those feelings come up, take a moment and treat yourself with compassion. Lay a hand on your heart and talk to yourself like you would to a good friend, giving yourself the words you need to hear.

There's another truth here as well, though: *You don't have to keep following these rules.* You can choose. You can find freedom within yourself separate from the rules you've been handed. That is grounded wildness.

CHAPTER 3

Glimpses of Wildness

Even during my strongest years of performing, I never completely lost myself. My colors were muted and my volume was turned down, but the bold, smiling girl holding the snake was still alive within me. Throughout these years, there were glimpses of wildness, times when that little girl emerged from hibernation and came out to play.

When I was a senior in high school, our entire tennis team decided not to return to school after we lost in the first round of our regional tournament. I wouldn't say our coaches endorsed the decision, but they knew we were doing it. This was such a common practice that it didn't feel like we were skipping school, but we were.

We got caught. And I was one of the captains of the team.

As part of our punishment, the high school athletic director asked me and the other captain to write a letter to our coaches "apologizing for our insubordination."

Let me pause here and tell you this: I HATE the word *insubordination*. Always have. I think it's the wildness in me that rebels against the very notion of insubordination. Even when I worked in human resources and insubordination was an infraction written in our employee handbook, I refused to use the word. I'd write down what someone did to receive the warning, but I'd never write them up for insubordination.

Now, back to the story.

First, let me paint a picture of my co-captain. She was basically the junior-year version of me. I was president of the National Honor Society. She would succeed me as president the next year. She was at the top of her class, just like me. Captain of multiple sports. All the things.

Simply put, we were good kids. We were nice, did what we were told, and were high-performing students and people, both in the traditional sense and in the ways I've described in this book.

Until someone asked us to apologize for our insubordination. At that moment, we became powerful, wild, and *grounded* in our conviction. Instead of cowering, we wrote a letter back to the athletic director explaining why we would *not* apologize for our insubordination, being careful not to throw our coaches under the bus in the process. We conceded to serve our detention, but we would not apologize.

We never heard back from our athletic director. Looking back, I don't think he had any idea what to do with us. We were the least likely kids to make an example of.

Or, perhaps he sensed there was no point in trying to negotiate with two women who were secure in their wildness, even if they were only sixteen and seventeen years old.

Then there were the five years after I graduated from college. I had no intention of following a traditional career path and instead taught environment education in New England, led gap year semesters in Central and South America, and led outdoor summer trips with teenagers in the American West and Costa Rica.

At that point, many of my high school friends were getting married, buying houses, and thinking about having kids. I had no permanent address, no consistent salary, and no aim to get married anytime soon. I was untethered from commitment and following my heart. Grounded wildness slinked just beneath the surface, trying to make an outright appearance. But it couldn't overtake the shame the rules had placed on me. Not yet, anyway.

Throughout my corporate years, there were moments when my grounded wildness surged to the surface, even after my voice had been quieted. I'd ask a challenging question, disagree with a leader, or propose a new way of doing things, my voice speaking directly from a grounded and wild place within me.

Nothing, though, captures those glimpses of wildness

quite like a blog post I wrote several years ago called "*La Via-jera*." The article described how a woman felt when traveling and how her wild spirit came to the surface when she was in far-flung corners of the world. While I wrote the piece in the third person, all the experiences and feelings I described were mine. *La Viajera* was me, a description of the grounded wildness I felt simmering in my soul but could not access in my day-to-day life. I called her *La Viajera*, the Spanish word for "woman traveler," because the English words I used in my regular life didn't quite seem to fit.

Here she is, in all of her grounded wildness:

> *La Viajera* turns her face toward the light. Her auburn hair glows in the rays of the sun and dances in the wind. She turns off the path and sits on a rock next to the river, setting her backpack beside her. She tugs off her hiking boots, peels her socks from her feet, and plunges them into the icy water. A thundering roar upstream catches her attention, and she turns with just enough time to see a glacier calving into the river up the valley from her resting stop.

> Her legs are depleted, but her soul is re-plenished. Here, she is free. She is surrounded by new landscapes, and the journey is the destination for her soul. She lies back, the warmth of the rock contrasting with the near-freezing water rushing past her feet. She relaxes fully into the sunshine, breathing it in and radiating the light back out into the world around her.

La Viajera has had this feeling before. It was fully present as she wandered the path hanging on the edge of cliffs on the Basque coast of Spain. She laughed with friends as they hiked, enjoying that they didn't know exactly where they were going. The small town in the river valley at the end of the trail was a beautiful surprise. A one-euro boat taxi led them to a lunch of wine and freshly caught fish.

And again, when she rented a bike in southern France and cycled along farm roads through vineyards. *La Viajera* got lost more times than she could count in that afternoon of biking. The kindness of strangers and multifaceted communication in English, French, gestures, and smiles reminded her of what is good in this world.

And once again, when she explored the temples of Angkor Wat with a friend. They wandered without a guide, turning corners and moving toward whatever captured their fancy. Curiosity drove their path forward.

But *La Viajera*'s mind is not on any of those experiences. Right now, she is lying in the sun on a rock next to a river, eyes closed and heart beating in tune with the pulse of the earth beneath her.

During my years of performing, I had to travel thousands of miles away from home to let *La Viajera* loose. The wonder and glory and the unknowns of travel practically forced my grounded wildness out of its shell and made *La Viajera* come out and play.

You know from reading these stories that *La Viajera* occasionally showed up in my day-to-day life as well. But those glimpses of wildness were most often followed by me wondering if I'd said too much, taken up too much space, or hurt someone's feelings by sharing my opinion directly. They were followed by the unsettling feeling that I might have shown too much of myself and the fear that *I* might be too much. It was a clash of the vulnerability of letting myself free— and the rules that told me I shouldn't be so free.

And then you get tired. Tired of the weight of the armor you're wearing, no matter how pretty and perfect it may look. Tired of every single one of the rules you're carrying on your shoulders. Tired of the work required to keep up appearances. Tired of constriction, constraint, and contraction. Tired of performing your life.

That's when you break.

Reflection Questions

1. When did you first lose your wildness?

2. What other experiences in your life caused you to constrict yourself and perform?

3. How do you perform? Do you prove, please, perfect, or rebel? Or do you do some of each?

4. What glimpses of wildness have you experienced? When has your version of *La Viajera* risen to the surface and made an appearance? How have those experiences made you feel?

—Part Two—

The Break

CHAPTER 4

Stay Awake

Remember the spring of 2020? It may seem like a blur now, the days running together in a haze of fear, uncertainty, Zoom gatherings, and staring at the interior walls of your house. But you remember. The world was breaking apart. Our ways of living had turned upside down overnight. Everything that felt normal had been ripped out from underneath us.

In the midst of this collective break, I wrote this poem, "Stay Awake," about my own breaking open:

> When you feel a crack inside of your soul,
> Slow down, pry it open, dive into the hole.

Sink, swallow, and let your truth thrive,
This is where you are most alive.

Shed the layers that kept you from hearing your heart,
Take a moment and listen to your whole in the parts.

Find freedom in allowing your feelings to flow,
Nothing held back, you can let it all show.

Stay awake for the wonder, the chaos, the pain,
Stay awake for it all, let go of the shame.

See the light shining from deep in your soul,
Nothing to fix, you were already whole.

So when the going gets tough, let tough be your guide,
Dive into your depths, that's where magic resides.

This is the break.

You break when you wake up to the rules you've been following. You break when the suffocation of constricting yourself into who you are supposed to be turns into a weight greater than you can bear. You break when you realize you can't keep performing for the rest of your life, when you discover that being a good girl isn't the path you want, when you realize that nodding your head and staying quiet when everything in you wants to SCREAM, simply is not going to happen anymore.

You break when you become awake to it all—and can stay

awake *through* it. When you can sit with your wonder, chaos, and pain and learn from the messages they send you. When you can dive into your depths and be with everything you find within you.

The break is both awful and wonderful. Beautiful and harrowing. It's questioning, grief, freedom, and joy all rolled into one. It's feeling yourself shattering into a million pieces while knowing the only thing that's shattering is the armor you've been wearing for far too long. It's breaking apart to realize you were never broken in the first place.

When you break, you may not know exactly what to do, but you are finally awake to it all. You are awake to your years of rebellion and conformity. Awake to how you've been pushing and forcing for so long. Awake to how you've been living outside your fullest truth and denying your complete nature. Awake to how you've had questions, but haven't really *questioned*. Awake to how you've trusted others' voices more than the voice inside of you.

You're awake to the possibility that you might just be enough, worthy, whole, and possibly even *radiant* without any performing at all.

The break is the opening to grounded wildness.

I've had multiple small breaks in the last several years. Quitting my corporate job to start my business was a break. Moving from Minnesota to Colorado was a break. Reconnecting to my spirituality separate from my Lutheran upbringing was a break.

You might be reading this list and thinking, *Wait. These are the SMALL breaks? Those all seem like pretty major life changes to me.*

And they were. But the break isn't about a major change on the *outside*; it's about a major change on the *inside*. In my life, I've only had two BIG breaks—at least so far. In the following pages, you'll read the details of each of these breaks, as well as the steps needed to break down, open, and *through* into your own grounded wildness.

CHAPTER 5

Break #1

My first book, *An Overachiever's Guide to Breaking the Rules*, is essentially a 184-page description of my first break.

Up to this break, I had always been an overachiever. An overdoer. The first one to raise my hand to volunteer for *anything*, from a work project to hosting a party. The one who pushed through workouts, injuries, and exhaustion, even when my body was pleading with me to just *stop* and *rest*. The one who felt like everything I did in school, work, and business had to be successful the very first time I tried it. The one who often felt on edge with the pressure she put on herself—like she might crumble and fall apart, if only she would allow herself to slow down and do it.

Then I finally stopped to ask myself why.

I was a year into running my business, doing all the things I was "supposed to" do to be a successful coach and entrepreneur: all the social media, Facebook ads, online courses, group programs, emails, and probably ten more things I don't remember because they've fallen so far off my radar in how I approach my business now.

Even more than the sheer number of tasks (which were overwhelming in themselves), it was the *way* I was doing them and the pressure I applied to force them to be successful. Every time I launched something new, I felt like it *had* to be THE thing. Like I needed this *one* thing to make my business a success.

I listened to all the experts, voraciously consumed business podcasts, and valued their opinion above anything I felt inside myself. Even though I was legally my own boss, I did as I was told by these experts, continuing my years of performing.

I was exhausted—not just physically, but also mentally, emotionally, and spiritually. I went to sleep thinking about Facebook ads, and they would reappear in my thoughts the second I woke up. At one point, I got on a call with my digital marketer and cried for over an hour just a few days before Christmas. I remember thinking that I had started my business to experience *more* freedom—and there I was, experiencing *less*.

The break came when I finally asked myself *why* I was doing all of this—and I slowed down long enough to listen to the answer.

It came to me immediately. I was doing it to prove myself. For two-and-a-half decades, I had connected my worth to achievement without consciously knowing it. I had swallowed the messages served by our culture that you always have to do more, build bigger, and move faster. I had pushed myself to excel at everything in school, work, business, and any kind of leadership to make up for the areas of my life where I felt like I could never be enough (in particular, my body, men, dating, sex, and motherhood, or lack thereof).

Over the following months, I unraveled these stories. I created a new belief that I am worthy for who I am, not what I do. I learned that doing less doesn't make me less. I can fail without being a failure—and success doesn't make me more of a person.

As I dismantled these old beliefs, my freedom grew. I stopped listening to the experts and started listening to myself. I completely changed the way I ran my business, stopping the ads, Facebook groups, and marketing funnels and instead focusing on speaking my truth, sharing what I had learned, and connecting with people on a deeply human level. I gradually let go of how I was "supposed to" present myself and just let myself present. As me.

That was when I wrote *An Overachiever's Guide to Breaking the Rules*. I don't know that I ever thought I had it *all* figured out. But at the time, I thought I had figured out a lot. This first break *was* huge for me. It fundamentally changed my life.

Little did I know that a bigger break was coming soon. A break that got to the root cause of it all. A break that finally allowed me to let go of the shame, see the light shining from deep in my soul, and believe I had nothing to fix and was already whole. The break that led me into my grounded wildness.

CHAPTER 6

Break #2

For even longer than I connected my worth to achievement, I was ashamed of my body. When I gained weight in seventh grade, the world told me that I was ugly—and that I was responsible for that ugliness. I got the message that I just needed a little more willpower and the right diet plan, and then I would regain my beauty—and my worth.

I wanted so badly to perform to this standard. I longed to meet the expectations of beauty laid out by our culture. And I tried! So hard! I counted calories, boxes, and points to constrict my eating. I spent hours on the StairMaster and NordicTrack, sometimes going to the extreme of attempting to burn off all the calories I had consumed that day or staying on the machine until the ticker reached a whopping 1,000 calories.

This was the one place in my life where I couldn't con-form, however. I didn't know how. All my efforts to perform would melt away the second I was consumed by a binge, downing hundreds—if not thousands—of calories in a single sitting. This, in turn, caused more shame as I wondered what was wrong with me. Why could everyone else manage their eating and I couldn't? What was I missing? What did I need to fix inside myself?

At one point, my parents talked to me about their concern over my weight. They did so in an appropriate way and from a place of love. In the moment, though, all I could do was fight against their concern. I either said or thought (the words feel so vivid in memory, but I suspect they didn't actually come out of my mouth), "I am PERFECT in every other area of my life. Can't you just GIVE ME THIS?!"

Even that response was full of shame. I didn't want to give myself this one area of imperfection, either.

The shame I felt in my body translated into how I showed up with boys in school, and then with men when I was an adult. I was always interested in guys; they just weren't interested in me. I also drove away the few who were interested before we could legitimately date. I was confident in so many areas of my life, but the second I drifted into any territory related to my body or romantic relationships, that confidence dis-integrated into thin air. I became scared and ashamed of how my belly looked—or, heaven forbid, that anyone might touch the rolls around my stomach.

Fairly quickly, I started assuming that any guy

I was interested in wouldn't like me as more than a friend. Despite this assumption, I hoped some guy would finally see the light and look at me. I clung to romantic comedies, yearning for the Bridget Jones moment when Mr. Darcy looks at her and says, "I like you. Very much. Just as you are." I wrote terrible poems about my longing to be noticed. I quite literally prayed that my current crush would want to be my boyfriend. I wanted it more than anything. Maybe even more than the number one slot in my class rank. (Maybe. I'm not sure about that one.)

My longing didn't align with what I thought I was worthy of, though. So I proved. You already got an overview of my proving in chapter 2. I would try to prove my worthiness by achieving and adventuring. I would point out everything we had in common. I would smile and laugh, even when I didn't get the joke. I would try to be perfect at everything else to make up for the shame I felt in my body and my perceived lack of desirability.

Over the years, the shame in my body expanded to include shame in my lack of relationship and sexual experience, which was a direct byproduct of said body shame. This area became just another place where I was falling short, another place where I was broken, another piece of evidence that I wasn't desirable.

Throughout those years, another pattern emerged: Guys I wanted to date would become interested in my friends. It started in eighth grade, when a guy I liked invited me to play tennis. I was *so* excited, thinking this was a sure sign he liked me.

At the end of our game, he asked if we could bike over to my friend's house to see if she—my pretty, thin friend—was at home. My stomach sank with dread. *Oh*, I thought. *He doesn't want to be here with me. He's here to get closer to HER*.

He later confirmed the story that had been running through my head: He liked me as a person. He enjoyed chatting with me in class and joking around. But as a girlfriend? Nope. That role was reserved for my friend.

Different versions of this pattern continued to repeat themselves over the next twenty-five years. I felt unchosen. Unseen. Completely invisible. Over and over and over.

So the proving continued. Over and over and over.

Then, one day, I did feel seen. I met someone who recognized me as a woman right away. He noticed all the parts of me I had always wanted someone to acknowledge, but didn't know how to bring forward. He took me out of the mirage of invisibility and pointed a spotlight directly at me, in the best way possible.

I felt desirable. Even more so, I felt free. He created a space where it was safe for me to bring my wildness forward. In fact, he *encouraged* me to bring it forward. He liked my big, fiery energy and wanted even more of it. I didn't have to prove anything to him; I just got to be me. I'd never experienced that before.

It didn't last long.

A month or two after we met, he told me he wasn't ready to be in a real relationship. My heart sank when he made this declaration. I knew an uber-casual relationship wasn't what I wanted, but I was enjoying this experience so much that I told him it was fine for now. It wasn't a lie—but it wasn't the complete truth either.

After he made his intentions known, my proving started to creep back in. I'd get nervous whenever he didn't text back right away. I'd check my notifications to see if the little word "Read" was listed below my message to see if he had, in fact, seen it and just didn't want to respond. I'd post pictures on social media, hoping he'd notice them and see what an awesome human I was—and that he should want to be with me! I fantasized with desperation, playing out a myriad of scenes in my head of us ending up together.

The more desperate I got, the more I proved.

The more I proved, the more he pulled away.

I knew he wasn't interested. I was disappointed and hurt, and I wanted so many things to be different.

But that didn't initiate the break.

This did: He texted me to say he was dating someone else.

The news BROKE ME. With that single text, a volcano of insecurity erupted. Every old story about my lack of desirability made an appearance. Every one of my vulnerable places felt exposed. Every one of my beliefs about never being chosen surged to the surface in an instant.

I broke. Completely. I felt like my entire being was an open wound that someone was continuously pouring salt into.

The feelings were so big, I had to actively release them—or I feared I might explode. I cried, then walked, then danced, then wrote, then called a friend and cried to her. Whenever I stopped these activities, I started to cry again. The continual release was required for me to make room for the ongoing onslaught of emotions.

I was so overcome that I was confused. Yes, I felt rejected by this man. Yes, when he told me he was dating someone else, he broke the last straw of hope I had been desperately holding on to that we would end up together. Yes, I was disappointed and hurt.

My reaction was caused by WAY more than just this guy, though. I was feeling thirty years of emotions surfacing all at once. It was a flood of rejection, hurt, fear, and shame, pouring out of every fiber of my being.

My heart was broken because *I* felt broken.

I knew I needed more help than what I could give myself. Something had to change. I needed to finally get to the root of where my proving was coming from and figure out how to change my beliefs and stories. I needed to be free.

I reached out to my health insurance company to inquire about coverage for therapy. It was covered, but there was a wait of several months to see anyone. Clearly, that wasn't going to work. I needed to see someone NOW.

Thankfully, I had the financial privilege to pay for therapy on my own, so I researched online companies and chose one that had good reviews. Then I did my best to circumvent the entire matching process by researching therapists and selecting my own. When the therapist I wanted was fully booked and I had no other choice but to succumb to the algorithm, I wrote an impassioned plea that my potential future therapist would read. My appeal stated that I had already done a ton of personal development work, I was a trained life coach, and I needed someone to dig in deep with me. No low-hanging fruit here, people!

Was this letter slightly arrogant, with undertones that I may know more than the therapist the algorithm would match me with? Perhaps. But this letter got me Mel.

Mel had everything I was looking for in a therapist, plus more I didn't know I needed. I got on our first video call and told her I didn't understand what was going on with me. Through tears, I explained I'd been doing everything I could to treat myself with compassion and release my emotions and they JUST KEPT COMING. The torrent would not stop.

After my sobbing, blubbering confessional, Mel looked at me with kind eyes and told me something I will never forget: "Releasing isn't the same as healing."

She was right. Feeling and releasing emotions is critical, but all the releasing in the world wasn't healing my underlying beliefs. Crying, writing, and dancing were all I could do in the midst of the onslaught, but they didn't dissolve the broken rules I'd been taught about what makes a woman worthy. They didn't get underneath the layers of shame I had been living with for decades.

I had broken down, and I was starting to break open. But I hadn't broken *through*. The rules I'd let go of when I disconnected my worth from achievement during my first big break were a starting point, but there was more work to do. It was like I had put back together one section of the puzzle, but this whole other section was a messy pile of pieces that were still scattered about.

It was time to put them back together. It was time to heal ALL of me. It was time to believe I was worthy, whole, and enough. It was time to rediscover my freedom.

CHAPTER 7

Break Down

I've had countless breakdowns in my life that never led to breaking open or breaking through. Those breakdowns related to both overachieving and the messy conglomeration of shame connected to my body, men, sex, and the cultural standard of what is considered desirable.

On the overachieving side, there was the time in high school when I completely broke down after finding out I'd been scheduled to interview for a fantastic mentoring program on the morning of the one day I had to sleep in over many weeks. Despite my excitement about this program, I didn't know how I could keep going without getting more sleep. Upon reading the letter advising me of the interview, I crumpled onto the kitchen floor and sobbed.

My mom found me there and fixed the situation on my behalf. She made me quit my job at church, allowing me to sleep in every Sunday. I didn't protest.

There was also a finals week in college, when I had a fever for an entire week and almost blacked out during one of my finals—only to have all of my "flu" symptoms disappear within a few hours after my last test was finished. I was sick, all right. But the root cause wasn't physical. It was pure stress and accumulated pressure from the rules I was following.

Then there was the wake-up call that should have been THE wake-up call: getting shingles when I was just thirty years old. I was so mired in the rules that told me I had to be productive, didn't need any help, and had to be successful that I didn't even take a single day off work. I didn't feel like I had a choice. I *had* to show up at work, keep performing, and keep feeding the bond between achievement and my worth. I'd been living by these rules for so long that it didn't occur to me I could make a different decision.

Then there's the other kind of breakdowns I experienced: those related to dating, men, and my perceived desirability. Yikes. PLENTY of breakdowns there as well. I've shed more tears, filled more journal pages, and endured more agony over men who were never interested in me than I would ever care to admit.

There was one breakdown that hit me particularly hard. It was yet another time when I was interested in a guy and he was interested in my friend. When she told me they were dating, I broke down. With FORCE.

For well over a month after getting the news, I'd find myself suddenly sobbing while walking to work, while sitting at home alone, or any other time I had space to think. A pit of dread would appear out of nowhere, lodging itself in my belly and remaining there, unwelcome, until it was distracted away.

To make matters worse, I saw these friends *all the time.* I was constantly reminded of the rejection. Constantly seeing their happiness. Constantly wanting to scream, but instead putting on a happy face in front of all our friends, the majority of whom had no idea how I was feeling.

I felt the crack inside of my soul, but I didn't slow down, pry it open, or dive into the hole. I sat with the pain, but nothing else changed. My internal narrative stayed the same.

Even more than that, this new rejection *reinforced* my story of not being desirable. Having yet another man choose my friend over me simply doubled down on my shame and gave me evidence that it was true.

The only questions running through my head were from my inner critic, spouting mean inquiries like, *Why don't men choose me? What do I need to do differently to get men to notice me? WHAT IS WRONG WITH ME?*

These were the wrong questions to ask. Their answers only led back to shame and the beliefs that I was undesirable and had to prove my worth. They guided me back to the broken rules I'd been taught about what makes a woman worthy and deserving. The pain of the situation had opened a crack in my soul, but these self-blaming questions caused that crack to snap shut, taking me right back to performing.

Different questions were needed for me to truly break *open*.

CHAPTER 8

Break Open

Breakdowns happen when some circumstance creates a change that gives you no other choice but to stop and deal with the emotions and questions coming up for you. Maybe you're exhausted. Maybe you got laid off. Maybe you're facing divorce. Maybe you found yourself answering emails yet again at 10:00 p.m. and wondered what the hell you were doing. Maybe you got sick. Maybe you had daughters and saw some of the rules you learned passed down to them. There are a million possibilities that can trigger a breakdown.

So often when we break down, we turn to self-judgment, just as I did. Throughout my life, I repeatedly asked myself some version of "What is wrong with me?"

The line of questioning didn't come *exactly* like that, though. It was more like this:

- Ugh. Here I am again, completely overcommitted. Why can't I learn to say no?! Why can't I set better boundaries once and for all?! (Implied: WHAT IS WRONG WITH ME?)

- Why did I eat that entire loaf of bread?! Now I feel sick. And ashamed. And like I should have learned how NOT to do this a million years ago. (Implied: WHAT IS WRONG WITH ME?)

- Why can't I just feel good in this bikini regardless of what my body looks like? I *know* the only reason I feel self-conscious is because of stupid rules the patri-archy taught me about what a woman who wears a bikini is "supposed to" look like—and I still feel this way! Why can't I just get over it?! (Implied: WHAT IS WRONG WITH ME?)

- Why am I thinking about this guy who I know isn't interested in me? Why do I keep holding out hope for something to change?! My God, I'm not a teen-ager anymore! Why can't I just get past it?! (Implied: WHAT IS WRONG WITH ME?)

These were (and sometimes still are) my self-judgment ques-tions. I have no doubt you have your own versions. These questions feel like they come from inside you, but they don't. They are a byproduct of the rules you were taught. They come out of the notion that you have to be productive and perfect and thin. That you aren't allowed to make a mistake. That you always have to do your absolute best and give 100 percent, no matter what. That you have to take care of everyone and be responsible for everything. That you aren't allowed to disappoint anyone. Ever.

Breaking open requires a different line of questioning.

You break open when you get curious with self-compassion, rather than with self-judgment. You explore what is going on with a neutral, open approach. You ask how your experiences and feelings connect to cultural expectations and bias. You notice how your shame relates to what you've been taught about how you are "supposed to" be and all the things you "should" do. You look at your patterns and take an honest dive into what needs to change. You hold yourself accountable for what is your responsibility—without thinking it's all on you.*

This compassionate approach to questioning led me through my first break when I disconnected my worth from achievement. With previous breakdowns, I felt like I just needed better boundaries or had to push through a little longer and then I could take a rest. I did little to explore what was happening below the surface; and when I did dip my toes into that water, I allowed for almost no self-compassion.

When I finally stopped to ask myself with open curiosity, "Why am I doing this? Why am I overdoing everything

---

*   You may do this exploration with a therapist, a good friend, or on your own through activities like journaling, meditation, and quiet walks—or a combination of all of this! Listen to yourself to determine the support you need.

and feeling all this pressure to succeed?"—that was when things started to change. I had an initial answer (I was doing it to prove myself); and from there, I could continue exploring.

Once I started investigating, I saw the near-constant messages we get that connect our worth to productivity and success. It was the Instagram post that read, "I'm living off two hours of sleep, four cups of coffee, and a dream." It was the business success stories that celebrated hitting six or seven figures, regardless of the health and well-being of the business owner or their employees. It was all the times I saw people being praised for working late, going above and beyond, and being an extraordinary team player— all while sacrificing their happiness, relationships, free time, and general aliveness.

Those *external* messages were easy to see once I opened my eyes, which made it easier to make *internal* changes. During this first break, I didn't need a therapist to help me break open and through. I was able to separate myself from the hustling rules our culture disseminates and choose a new set of rules to live by on my own. I adopted the belief of "I am worthy for who I am, not what I do." Within a few months, I noticed significant shifts. The pressure to make my business a success loosened. I felt healthier in every sense of the word. The breaking open and breaking through continued, but I quickly found a newfound freedom within myself and had no plans to give it back.

Breaking open the second time around required more exploration and vulnerability. When I stopped to ask myself questions, there were no immediate answers like there had been during my first break. I felt good about most parts of myself, but this one piece related to my body and desirability was completely shattered. The pieces were so broken that I didn't know how to start putting them back together.

That was why I sought help to guide me during this process of breaking down, open, and through. Not just through therapy with Mel (as I mentioned earlier), but also through talking with friends who could listen and witness without judgment, reading books about the feminine and letting go of shame, and participating in services and small groups at a Unitarian Universalist (UU) church I'd recently started attending. I needed every single part of this support to help me keep embracing vulnerability and moving forward.

Breaking open is the space in between. It's asking questions without having immediate answers. It's shedding the layers that kept you from hearing your heart and leaving yourself bare. It's staying awake for the wonder, the chaos, and the pain. Breaking open requires you to stay awake for it all—and that is UNCOMFORTABLE.

In my experience, breaking open is the hardest part of the journey to grounded wildness. The word *open* itself implies vulnerability. You are in the liminal space between the old and the new. You've started to move away from all the rules that kept you small, but you haven't yet moved into a new way of being. No matter how ready you are to throw off the layers of suffocation and shame forever, it's unsettling.

Sink into it. Let the discomfort be there. Feel the restlessness. Feel the rumble inside of you. Let it be messy, vulnerable, and awakening all in the same moment. Let yourself cry, run, scream, dance, and laugh.

Feel the layers start to peel off. Recognize the old rules that are breaking down. See the glimpses of your wild self, even if she is still off in the distance. Notice the nudges of your true inner voice, whether they are a hard push with a clear message or nothing more than a barely audible whisper.

Then keep noticing. Keep asking compassionate questions. Keep diving into your depths. You're about to find out where your magic resides.

CHAPTER 9

Break Through

I've had multiple mini breakthroughs over the last several years, but only one true, thorough, deep breakthrough that forever altered the course of my life—and how I felt *in* my life.

I was in the middle of my second break, in deep therapy with Mel to unearth the shame related to my body, AND reading *Rising Strong* by Brené Brown. I came to the point in *Rising Strong* where Brené describes how the stories we create become patterns. Then our brain recognizes those patterns and jumps to conclusions. We feel so certain about these stories, but they are typically neither true nor accurate.

As I read her words, I felt something click into place. I decided to rewrite the story I'd learned as a teenager about my body and what makes a woman desirable.

Here's the old story:

Boys aren't interested in me because of my weight.

I'm ashamed of my weight and my body.

I'm ashamed of myself for not being able to control
my eating and lose weight.

I'm broken because I can't do these things for myself.
Because I can't fix myself.

Then I wrote a new story:

Boys aren't interested in me because of my weight.

Our culture tells women that their body is a key part of their
worth, desirability, and likability. In particular, that thin
is worthy, desirable, and likable.

Everyone, regardless of gender, absorbs these messages
about women's worth, doing a disservice to us all.

I'm not broken. The system is broken.

THAT'S IT.

I'm not broken. The *system* is broken.

Whoa.

BREAK *THROUGH*.

For my entire life, the system told me I was smart. An achiever. A leader. I leaned into those messages.

The system also told me my body was ugly and undesirable—and I leaned into those messages as well.

Connecting my worth to both sets of messages was a performance; a constant dance of proving myself. It was a battle that could never be won because the fight was based on faulty information.

The *real* truth is that I am worthy, whole, enough, and completely and totally RADIANT without having to do anything at all.

So are you. No proving, pleasing, perfecting, or rebelling needed.

You break through when you realize your performance is driven by trying to live up to standards that were always broken. Shame doesn't come from you; it comes from the gap between this broken standard and your reality. It's the distance between all the shoulds telling you how your body, gender, sexuality, skin color, hair, house, bank account, success, friends, family, vacations, performance review, salary, and a million other things are "supposed to" look versus how they actually look in your life.

Only, nothing was ever wrong with your body, gender, sexuality, skin color, hair, house, bank account, success, friends, family, vacations, performance review, or salary. Sure, we all have things to work on, but nothing was ever wrong with you.

You were never broken. *The system is broken.* The rules you were taught are broken.

Once you realize this, you suddenly see the light shining from deep in your soul. There's nothing to fix—you were already whole. You can come back to yourself, separate from the rules you were taught, separate from the weight of "should" and "supposed to." You no longer require approval or validation. You can stop performing and just BE.

This is freedom.

This is power.

This is grounded wildness.

Reflection Questions

1. What breaks (large or small) have you experienced in your life?

2. Where do you need to break away from performing in your life now?

3. What rules and stories have you been fed that have led you to proving, pleasing, perfecting, and rebelling in your life, like my stories connecting my worth to achievement and my likability and desirability to my body?

4. Take these rules and rewrite your story. Use the example I outlined from my own experience a few pages earlier. Give yourself a new ending—a truthful ending, one that breaks down the lies of those rules and gives you freedom.

Part Three

Grounded
Wildness

CHAPTER 10

Becoming the Leading Lady of Your Life

You know the movie *The Holiday*? It's one of my favorites. In the movie, Kate Winslet plays Iris, a woman strung along by an old boyfriend of whom she can't quite seem to let go. On a whim, she books a last-minute house swap over Christmas with Cameron Diaz's character, who lives in a gorgeous home in Los Angeles. Of course, romantic entanglements ensue for both of them, like any good romantic comedy should do.

Although I love the romantic storyline between Iris and Miles, played by Jack Black, what I'm most interested in here is Iris's break into her own grounded wildness. At one point early in the movie, Iris is having dinner with her spunky elderly neighbor when he comments that he can tell she's a leading lady, but she's been behaving like the best friend.

Through tears, Iris responds, "You're so right. You're supposed to be the leading lady of your own life, for God's sake."

This is the start of Iris's big break. Throughout the movie, you see Iris coming into her own and standing tall in her life. She had broken *down* for years, but she was about to break *open* and *through*.

Her moment of truth comes late in the movie, when Iris's schmucky ex shows up at her door while she's on vacation, saying that he misses her. At first, she acquiesces and lets him in. But then she starts asking questions. For the first time ever, she listens to her inner knowing, stands on the freedom of her worth, and stops performing. You see her letting go of shame as she tells him her truth. Instead of giving him the benefit of the doubt, she trusts herself, tells him that she has a life to start living, and kicks him out the door.

In the highlight of the movie for me, Iris's schmucky ex stands in the doorway, looking confused and asking what has gotten into her.

Iris responds with power and confidence, "I don't know, but I think what I've got is something slightly resembling *gumption*." Then she slams the door, throws her arms in the air, and realizes she is an entirely new woman.

A woman living in grounded wildness.

I am also Iris. For years, I felt like part of me was on the side-lines. You wouldn't have known it from the outside. I spoke up frequently. I made bold moves in my career, like moving to Australia for a year alone. I appeared pretty darn confident most of the time. I knew the fullness of me was missing, though. I knew that performing was holding me back. Shame had turned down the volume of my radiance, pushing me from leading-lady status to best friend.

Then I broke down, open, and through. I recognized the rules I'd been handed and the shame they had caused. I understood on a deep level that the system was broken, not me. With that realization came a freedom that went way beyond my body and overachieving and bled into all parts of my life. I immediately began turning my volume back up, inch by inch returning to the adult version of the little girl holding the snake.

Now, every part of me is on stage, but I'm not performing in some one-act play meant to keep others comfortable. I'm centered in exactly who I am—and all of who I am: the leading lady of my life, grounded and wild.

It sounds like a contradiction, doesn't it? Grounded wild-ness? How can you be both grounded and wild at the same time? Isn't being grounded the opposite of being wild?

No. In fact, it's the grounding that enables the wildness.

Years before I thought of this concept, while I was still mired in performing, I unknowingly wrote a description of grounded wildness in my journal. It bub-bled up on one of those days when I sensed my truest self shimmering beneath the surface, separate from the constraint the rules had endowed on me. It was yet another small glimpse of wildness. Here's what I wrote:

> I feel the inner and outer converging into one, and I know that I am whole. There is a grounding in my belly that is simultaneously heavy and free, like it's keeping me attached to the earth so that my imagination can run free and I don't have to worry about getting lost, about becoming unhinged. **I am free to be free, and I'll still be right here.**

During the years of performing, you are either conforming to the rules you've been handed by proving, pleasing, and perfecting your way through life, or actively pushing against them by rebelling. Both reactions are a constant swim upstream against your true nature. Both reactions require inordinate effort and diligence to keep up appearances. Both reactions take YOU away from YOU.

Breaking through into grounded wildness means that you get to let go of pushing *against* yourself and instead sink *into* yourself. You've awakened to the rules you've been handed about what a good woman is supposed to be and all the performing this definition has caused. You've realized you can choose to keep following those rules and carrying the weight of shame they induced—or you can let yourself free. You can stand wild in your freedom because you are grounded in your worth.

From the outside, grounded wildness may look like rebellion. A woman free from performing is often breaking the rules she's been taught. She's aligned with herself rather than conforming to what the world has told her she "should" be. She's following her path rather than the path prescribed for her. She speaks up and rocks the boat when something doesn't sit right. She upsets the status quo just by living in her freedom.

The difference between rebellion and grounded wildness isn't what you see on the outside, though. It's how it feels on the *inside*. Rebellion is breaking the rules for the sake of breaking the rules. It's going against the grain, even when you're going against yourself. It's taking the out-there job, being in a relationship with a free spirit, or dressing wildly because it's unexpected, not because it feels like you.

In rebellion, you are *rising up against*. In grounded wildness, you are *sinking into*. This is freedom.

It doesn't matter if people call you a rebel, a strong independent woman, direct, aggressive, or too much. It doesn't matter if they say those words with a smile and a tone of admiration or with a condescending look and an attitude of judgment. You know how it feels on the inside. You know if you are rebelling or simply living as your full self, free in your grounded wildness.

The opposite is true as well.

You might assume a stay-at-home mom living in the suburbs who spends her time cooking, organizing the family, and taking care of her home is the height of proving, pleasing, and perfecting. And she might be.

Or, that life might just be her. She may know that being a mother and managing her home is her ultimate calling. With that knowing, she can discard the rules she's gotten telling her that being a stay-at-home mom isn't enough and she should also have a high-powered career and be killing it in the board room AND the kitchen. (And be a sex goddess for her husband at night, because isn't that the ultimate superwoman?!)

Being a stay-at-home mom in the suburbs isn't my version of living in grounded wildness, but it might be hers. The point is, you can't tell from the outside. Only you can know for yourself on the inside.

That's because grounded wildness comes from the inside. Period. When you are living in grounded wildness, there are times when you will align with the norm, but you won't be conforming. There will be times when you will buck the status quo, but you won't be rebelling. Instead, you will listen to yourself for the right path. You will trust your inner voice more than the external voices around you. You will validate yourself instead of twisting your decisions according to others' opinions.

Because of that, grounded wildness may look and feel differently for you than it does for me. I'm not suggesting that you follow my path. I'm suggesting that you follow *your* path.

I'm suggesting that you look at the rules you were taught and the shame they have caused, and start asking questions. I'm suggesting that you let yourself break down those old rules, break open to the possibility of a different way of living, and break through to freedom, whatever that looks like for you.

I'm suggesting that you become the leading lady of your life.

A Quick Note about What Grounded Wildness Is Not

Before we continue, I want to share a few important clarifications about what grounded wildness is *not*.

Grounded wildness is *not* thinking you have it all figured out or never need feedback from anyone. In fact, I believe that grounded wildness makes you *more* open to change and feedback. When you have nothing to prove, you have nothing to protect. You can be open to learning and doing better because your worth isn't attached to already doing it perfectly. You can do things differently because you aren't dependent on external validation praising you for repeating what you've always done well. When the veil of performing lifts, you are free to listen, evolve, and do better the next time.

Grounded wildness is also *not* about blaming the system for everything and shirking all personal accountability. You are responsible for your actions and decisions—and you realize there is usually a systemic component influencing those actions and piling a "should" onto your decisions. You acknowledge the impact of the roles you were forced to play to survive and the ways you had to perform to succeed in your family, school, culture, and workplace—*and* you take responsibility for your patterns and make a different choice now.

What's more, when you recognize the impact of culture, then you can look at your actions with compassion. You can get curious about your patterns instead of shaming yourself for repeating the same mistake. You can investigate why you've shown up in certain ways without condemning yourself. You can see your role and take accountability for your decisions without taking on the weight of everything that went wrong with the relationship, the project, the conversation, etc.

Grounded wildness is also *not* about being happy all the time or everything being easy. While I believe there is a certain ease to living in alignment with yourself, I'm not a fan of the messages declaring you can get everything you want without any hardship as long as you really believe they are possible and don't let any negative thoughts enter your psyche. Messages like this ignore the realities of culture and life. They disregard financial hardships, discrimination, illness, and conflict. They are tied in with toxic positivity and white privilege.

Grounded wildness is not about manifesting your perfect life and living in bliss every moment of the day. It's about being *alive*. It's about disconnecting from the rules and reconnecting to the freedom breathing inside you. It's about feeling everything from despair to serenity and the entire spectrum in between. It's about staying awake for the wonder, the chaos, AND the pain.

All of it. All of YOU. Living out loud in this world.

CHAPTER 11

The Four Tenets of Grounded Wildness

A t its core, the move from performing to grounded wildness is about shifting the beliefs you have about yourself. It's about getting rid of the notion that you are either not enough or too much and realizing you were always worthy and whole, with no performing required.

Transforming your beliefs is the difference between simply breaking down and truly breaking through. If you break down without changing your beliefs, you go back to performing. If you break down, open, and through to a new belief system, you move toward grounded wildness.

I've discovered four tenets at the heart of grounded wildness. These beliefs have guided me to (mostly) let go of proving, pleasing, perfecting, and the occasional rebelling, and to reconnect to the grounded, wild woman I am. Leaning into these beliefs has released shame and its accompanying proving and allowed me to just show up. As me. All of me.

I believe these tenets in my soul. They've become a part of me, a current running beneath the surface that's guiding my actions, my decisions, and how I show up in the world. Perhaps most importantly, they've changed the way I *feel* about how I show up in the world. They've altered the entire energy of my being. They've given me freedom. They've changed my life. Forever.

Tenet #1: You Were Never Broken. You Are Innately and Completely Enough, Worthy, and Whole

This is the number one tenet for a reason: It is the heart of grounded wildness. The life-giving, soul-loving core of your freedom.

When you believe any part of you is broken, you are in a constant race to prove your worth. You exhaust yourself in an attempt to perfect your way to being enough and please your way to wholeness. It's a race that can never be won because *the race doesn't exist*. You can't *prove* your worthiness because you simply *are* worthy.

For the most part, our culture tells you the opposite. Our world gives you subtle and not-so-subtle messages about what is acceptable, good, and successful. It pushes you to believe it's your fault if you're not meeting those expectations. It tells you that you are broken and need to be fixed. It warns you that the race is completely real, and you better keep running or you'll just fall farther behind.

This isn't a problem with you. It's a problem with the system.

You were never broken. *The system* is broken.

This realization was one of the biggest aha moments I've ever had. It exploded through my body, immediately releasing shame. A dark, heavy cloak lifted from my shoulders, never to weigh me down again.

I saw how the messages I'd gotten about what a woman's body should look like were flat-out wrong. I looked at hustle culture and the hamster wheel of productivity through new eyes and realized they were completely ridiculous. I understood the feedback I'd gotten about being too direct was less about my communication style and more about a larger system rooted in patriarchy that is meant to keep you in your place and maintain the status quo.

Think about it: If you believe your own brokenness is the root of your problems, what are you going to try and fix? Yourself. You are kept small in the confines of your shame and quiet in the assumption of your brokenness.

If you believe the system is broken, what are you going to try and fix? The system. You challenge rules, assumptions, and ways of living. You question decisions, and you aren't satisfied with any response that sounds like, "Well, that's the way we've always done it." You rock the boat and become the squeaky wheel, and *change happens*.

YOU break down, open, and through—and then the SYSTEM breaks down, open, and through. So be a revolutionary. Believe you are enough.

Tenet #2: You Belong Within

During the years of performing, there is a tendency to rely on other people to tell you if you're on the right path. You take the job recommended by your boss. You ask your friends when they think it's the right time for you to have kids. You take advice from all the experts about how you should run your business.

I'm not talking about being open to different perspectives, taking in feedback, or learning from others. I'm talking about trusting others' voices over the voice of your knowing. I'm talking about seeking validation for your decisions or polling people before making those decisions in the first place. I'm talking about relying on any entity outside of you to guide the direction of your life.

You do this because some part of you has been taught that you *don't* belong to yourself. You've been advised to ignore or distrust your inner voice. You've been instructed to disconnect from the signals your body is sending and keep driving forward, no matter whose path you are on. All these rules efficiently and effectively guide you away from belonging within.

When you break those rules and step into grounded

wildness, you realize you already have the answers inside you. Your body knows what it needs. You know your next career move. You know the right partner for you. You know what you're feeling. You know.

In grounded wildness, you understand that your power originates entirely inside of you. People and experiences can reveal parts of yourself you may not have been aware of before. They help you learn about yourself and challenge your thinking. But only you can give yourself permission to unleash everything you are and show it to the world. You validate your sense of completeness. You trust the voice inside of you more than the noise around you. You have faced, accepted, and *embraced* the truth of who you are. You are your own friend and ally.

This is belonging within.

Tenet #3: You Are Radiant

Take a deep breath. How did you feel when reading the words, "You are radiant"? If you skimmed past them, go back. Take a moment and let them sink in.

Do those words feel cheesy? Silly? Or *deeply* uncomfortable?

I'm guessing they feel more like the latter. They certainly did for me.

As I was brainstorming ideas for this book, I realized I was just as uncomfortable with the thought of sharing my stories of freedom as I was sharing my stories of brokenness. It's just as vulnerable for me to talk about all the things that make me amazing as it is to talk about my mistakes and faults. To be frank, it makes me nauseous to think of you reading some of the stories of my wildness that you'll find in the next chapter.

They aren't salacious or scandalous. They aren't even all that out there! Logically, I think you'll read them and say to yourself, "Why was she worried about this at all?"

I'll tell you why: Because it's exposing to step into the light when you've been shoving parts of yourself into the shadows for most of your life. It's hard to burst out of the box you've been placed in, even if you want nothing more than to rip up that box and light it on fire. It's uncomfortable to be a woman living in her fullness without apology when you've been told your entire life that there are parts of you that you should apologize for.

And yet, there's a light inside of you that cannot be extinguished. A flame that continues to glow no matter what rules are placed upon you. No matter what shame accumulates. No matter how many times, ways, and places you've been told to dull your light. Your fire keeps burning.

Breaking into grounded wildness allows that fire to burst from a flickering candle to a bonfire blaze. You begin to feel your radiance—and you start showing it to the world. People notice. Some are drawn to you. Others are curious. Still more are uncomfortable, not quite knowing what to make of a woman standing tall in her glory. A few are straight-up pissed off and ask, "Just who does she think she is?"

The beautiful thing about grounded wildness is that it doesn't matter. Your fire comes from inside of you. Neither praise nor contempt nor disinterest can take it away. You glow with spirit and aliveness. Your worthiness lights up the world.

You. Are. Radiant.

Tenet #4: You Get to Make Up Your Own Tenets of Grounded Wildness

I don't get to decide your beliefs about your grounded wildness. You do. That's why this final tenet is so important. You have the choice to throw away anything in this book that doesn't work for you and replace it with something that does. You have the freedom to add one, two, or five tenets to the three I listed so far in this chapter. You get to decide.

So ask yourself these questions: What beliefs are needed for you to feel free? What tenets will allow you to release shame and step into your radiance? What do you need to create your own rules for life? What is your inner voice whispering to you right now?

There is no right or wrong. There is only what feels good, aligned, and freeing to you. You don't even need to fully believe all your tenets right now. I didn't believe in my radiance for a long time, even when I could feel the desire to step into the light. The deeply embodied belief in your tenet will come eventually. The fourth part of this book, Getting Grounded and Wild, is filled with practices to move you in that direction.

So choose for *you*. What are your tenets?

CHAPTER 12

From Performing to Grounded Wildness: Four Stories

Story #1

I had no idea what I was doing when I started my business. This wasn't imposter syndrome—although I experienced some of that too! It was just a fact. I knew how to do the content of my work (coaching, training, and speaking), but I didn't know how to run a business. I'd never sold anything except babysitting services, never marketed a single product, and never even sent an invoice.

There was *a lot* to learn.

So I turned to the experts. I ravenously listened to business podcasts. I accepted all the things marketers told me I was supposed to do to have a successful online coaching business, like launching freebies, running ads, having a Facebook group, and growing my Instagram following.

I did as I was told. I followed the rules. I created programs and courses, and hired two separate digital marketers to launch those offerings. They told me about the quizzes and free webinars I needed to share to bring people into my email list. I followed their advice, just like I was supposed to. I recorded the videos they suggested for Facebook ads and created a million different email chains to target different groups, just like I was supposed to.

The problem was, I didn't like doing the things I was supposed to do. I hated running Facebook ads. Hated putting together all the different email chains. HATED feeling like I was supposed to use marketing language that hit on pain points and scarcity. Hated the stress leading up to launches and feeling like the effort had better be worth it or else I was a total failure.

Then my efforts did fail. Not just once, but *three* times. And not a slight failure that you could potentially learn from and adjust, but a complete and total bust. No one signed up for my programs. Three times over.

Thank *God*.

If they'd been successful, I might have gotten stuck running those Facebook ads and online marketing for many more years. I would have been miserable. So thank God they failed.

The final failure caused me to stop and ask myself,

"How do *I* want to run my business? How do I want to show up in the world? How do I want to connect with people? How do I want to create an impact? And, perhaps most importantly, what feels *good*? Where are my intuition and my true inner voice guiding me?"

Then I started doing things my way.

Fast-forward a few months. Instead of running ads, I started sharing posts on social media that felt like truth. I aimed to simply be a real person connecting with real people. I let go of the online programs and focused on speaking, where I found joy and impact.

Here's the fascinating thing: When I let go of all the things I was supposed to do to run a successful business, I had more success. When I stopped blindly following what other people were doing, started sifting through their advice to see what made sense for me, and began throwing everything else out the window, my business grew. When I started listening to myself over all the voices telling me how I *should* perform, things got a whole lot better.

Not just in the traditional sense—although my revenue and profits increased substantially as well—but in all aspects of success. Now, people reach out more often to let me know something I've shared on social media has made a difference for them. They tell me they feel seen and heard as an audience member when I speak and have made different decisions coming out of the event. I also have more time for hiking, exploring, and making snow angels, which are important parts of my definition of success as well.

I don't have to put on a performance of how a business

owner is supposed to look, what they're supposed to do, and how they're supposed to show up in the world. I can share my gifts, connect with people, and listen to my knowing for the next steps to take. That is enough.

This is grounded wildness.

Story #2

In 2009, I went through an extensive coaching training program. The trainers came from the Coaches Training Institute, but it was hosted by my company. I participated with thirty of my colleagues who also wanted to be internal coaches for leadership development programs and one-on-one executive engagements.

Throughout the four months of the program, we learned to coach by coaching each other. The instructors would demonstrate a coaching skill in front of the room, and then we would pair up and decide who was the coach and who was the client. The client would pick a topic they wanted coaching on and share it with their coach. The coach would then practice the coaching skill we had just learned in real time.

Basically, these thirty colleagues got to know my challenges, dreams, desires, and vulnerabilities *real* quick.

At one point, I decided I needed coaching on dating. Carol was my partner. I trusted her and felt like I could talk about this decidedly not-work-related topic in a one-on-one conversation. I'm also fairly certain I'd already cried in front of the entire room by this point, so what was one more vulnerable discussion?

Carol and I stood face-to-face in a large conference room surrounded by fifteen other pairs of colleagues who were also coaching each other. As Carol coached me, one of our trainers came alongside us and observed our conversation. At a pause, he whispered something in Carol's ear.

"What did you say?" I asked.

The trainer looked me right in the eye. "I said, 'Do you think Heather knows she's beautiful?'"

Everything in me sunk. A million different indescribable emotions arose at once, swirling in a pot of insecurity. The only specific thing I remember thinking was, *No. I don't know that I'm beautiful. No.*

It wasn't THE truth, but it was MY truth at the time. The rules I'd been taught about what beauty was supposed to look like had buried any notion of my beauty under the heavy weight of shame.

Fast-forward many years. I'm heart-deep in working with my therapist while coming out of my second big break. Together, we created a list of statements I wanted to believe about myself. I wrote the declarations in looping, casual cursive on a standard sheet of white paper, alternating each line between purple, pink, and blue ink. Then I taped the page on the bathroom mirror, a place where there would be no chance of me ignoring it.

I stared at myself in that mirror and began saying the lines out loud:

I am beautiful.

I am desirable.

I am worthy.

I am whole.

I see and accept myself fully.

I bring my full self to the world.

Tears misted in my eyes the first few times I said those sentences. Even though I didn't fully believe their words, there was something simultaneously compassionate, powerful, and vulnerable about looking at my reflection directly in the eye and telling myself that I am beautiful, desirable, worthy, and whole. That I see all of that in me—and I bring it to the world.

The tears disappeared after a few days. Soon, saying the lines felt neutral. There was a certain factualness in the process, but not yet a deep belief. Still, I looked at myself every day in the mirror and said with the most conviction I could muster:

I am beautiful.

I am desirable.

I am worthy.

I am whole.

I see and accept myself fully.

I bring my full self to the world.

Over the coming weeks, neutrality turned into belief. I started looking at myself in the mirror with a smile, sometimes even turning sideways and giving myself a downright flirtatious glance. I smirked and sassed my way through the lines, feeling their truth flow through my body:

I am beautiful.

I am desirable.

I am worthy.

I am whole.

I see and accept myself fully.

I bring my full self to the world.

I wasn't relying on another person to say these words to me. Of course, it feels good to hear those words from someone else, but I didn't require an external voice to tell me I was beautiful to believe it myself.

I saw my beauty in both a very physical way and on a deeper level. I saw my radiance.

This is grounded wildness.

Story #3

Over a decade ago, I was working on what is still the biggest project of my life. For six months, I was the project manager for two simultaneous in-person global leadership events at my company. I ate, breathed, and even slept (through stressful dreams!) those events. The work was unending. There was no human way to answer all the emails I received, yet they all felt important. At one point, I calculated that my twenty-year-old intern was making more money per hour than me. She was limited to forty hours a week. I was not.

I also got shingles during this project—something no otherwise-healthy thirty-year-old should get. I had no idea how to set boundaries. No idea how to question my workload. No idea how to stop proving, pleasing, and perfecting.

During this time, I often listened to a song called "Slightly Soiled" that my friend Nick had written and recorded. At its core, the song is about growing up. But there was one line that hit me in a deep spot when I was drowning in this project—and in performing. It went like this:

> I get lost inside the paper shuffle,
> I lose my grip and my feathers ruffle,
> but I'll never say a word.

At one point, I was listening to the song on my iPod while sitting in my cube, surrounded by piles of work I had no idea how I would complete. Tears came to my eyes as I realized the truth of those words in that moment of my life:

> I'll never say a word.

That was me. I might get lost, I might lose my grip, and my feathers might be ruffling all over the place, but I'll never say a word. I'll just smile, pretend it's all fine, and get back to work.

Fast-forward over a decade. I purposefully decided to work less for an entire summer. I was burned out from the pandemic and deep personal work, and I needed a break to recover. I needed some space to feel alive again.

In May of that year, I chose a theme song for the summer. This song fit my mood, my desires, and my entire approach to life for those three months. It matched the feelings of grounded wildness that were growing in my soul. And it was the complete opposite of getting lost inside the paper shuffle and never saying a word.

The song was "Wildflowers" by Tom Petty and the Heartbreakers, although I listened to The Wailin' Jennys's rendition. Those lyrics matched my new approach to work—and to my life as a whole.

I *did* belong somewhere I felt free. Not just for a summer, but for always. So do you.

This is grounded wildness.

Story #4

During my years of performing, I would occasionally meet a man who made me feel beautiful. And fun. And like he might be glimpsing the real part of me.

In those fleeting times, I felt free. The proving temporarily disappeared. I laughed with abandon. I flirted without questioning myself. I loosened my hips, danced, and downright sashayed with all the comfort and confidence in the world.

Despite the reality that these moments usually only lasted a single evening, my fantasies would typically kick into overdrive. I'd see the two of us falling in love, adventuring together, and loving life. I'd see myself blossoming under his care, finally breaking free and letting my full self out into the world. *He* held the key to unlock *my* magic.

I always wondered, *What is it about these particular guys, in these particular situations, that brings out this side of me? What is it about THEM that gives ME freedom?*

Fast-forward several years. I had a second date scheduled with a guy. The morning of that date, I woke up positively on *fire*. Instead of using one of my typical tea mugs, I grabbed my Double Trouble mug from Oktoberfest and drank my herbal tea out of it. It was the only thing that fit my mood. I was ready for fun—and I was going to *create* fun, no matter what.

Turns out I didn't have to create anything. I embodied

fun before I ever arrived to meet my date. I walked into our city adventure exploring the arts district with the self-assuredness of Beyoncé.

At one point, we were huddled under an umbrella, holding on to each other to avoid raindrops as we walked toward a brewery. I had an immediate desire to kiss him. Without questioning myself or thinking about his reaction, I stopped us in the middle of the sidewalk and said, "I think we should make out."

As you can imagine, he had no problem obliging that request!

In that moment, I realized the biggest secret of them all: The freedom I felt never came from those men. *It always came from me.* None of those men had the key to unlock my magic; only I held it. Like Dorothy clicking the heels of her red sequin shoes, the power was within me all along.

This is grounded wildness.

Reflection Questions

1. What does grounded wildness mean to you?

2. When you are both grounded and wild, how does that feel? What are the sensations in your body?

3. What beliefs are needed for you to feel free? Add these to your personal tenets of grounded wildness.

4. Reflect over the past several years of your life. What are your stories of going from performing to grounded wildness? Where have you already let go of a rule you were handed and stepped into your own freedom?

—Part Four—

Getting Grounded and Wild

A NOTE TO THE READER

The first three sections of this book were all about the who, what, why, where, and when of the journey to grounded wildness. You explored the years of performing and the ways you have proved, pleased, perfected, and rebelled your way through different parts of life. You read about my treks into breaking down, open, and through; and you reflected on the breaks in your own life. You leaned into grounded wildness and discovered the rooted freedom of its wings.

Now it's time for the *how*. Over the next several chapters, you'll uncover practices that will help you dismantle the rules you've been handed, move through the breaks, and continue on your journey to grounded wildness.

These are the practices that have worked for me—and that have resonated with many other people in my programs and audiences. I have no doubt you'll get value out of them, but they're not a perfect roadmap to grounded wildness. They're not a step-by-step framework you can cross off a to-do list and accomplish. The journey to your freedom isn't a straight line.

I invite you to try all the practices. Then, even more importantly, listen to yourself. Throw out the practices that don't work for you. Add in others that aren't in the book. Do what feels freeing and centering for you. Take the steps *you* need to move toward grounded wildness.

That itself is an act of grounded wildness.

CHAPTER 13

Create Space

At some point during the spring of 2021, I realized I needed a break. We were a full year into the pandemic by that time. On top of that, over the past six months, I had published my first book, I had moved to Colorado, and my business had exploded with growth. I was also in the midst of one of my breaks—and, as I said to my therapist at the time, I had underestimated the energy required for deep transformation.

It was all good. (Not the pandemic, but everything else.) It was also A LOT.

I needed to give myself permission to back off. I didn't want to take a full sabbatical, but I needed to work less for an extended time. I needed to rest until I didn't want to rest anymore. I needed to sit on my patio and look up at the sky. I needed to journal, take naps, and read by the lake. I needed to be quiet and listen to my true inner voice. I needed to tune into the ideas I felt starting to percolate inside me for this book.

In short, I needed space. And for the first time in my life, I took it.

I gave myself the entire summer to do less. I rarely set an alarm. Instead of waking up every weekday and automatically jumping on my computer, I asked myself each morning what I really needed and wanted to do that day, then followed the response to the best of my capability. I took cues from my curiosity when it came to what I worked on in my business. I still followed through on my commitments, but everything else was scaled back in a huge way. I created fewer social media posts, reached out less often to potential clients, and took every Friday off to go hiking.

I decided all of this in advance. I gave myself active, full, complete permission to do less.

Then I started doing it. Less, that is.

And it was *weird*.

Old rules showed up out of nowhere. The stories of my previous years of performing made a quick and determined appearance. They told me I should be doing more and working harder. They pushed me to take advantage of this time and be productive. They judged me directly, saying it was 9:00 a.m. on a Tuesday and that was the time for work—so I better get to it!

There were tinges of guilt. And more than a few moments

of discomfort. I fought against those feelings, trying my best to drop-kick the old rules in the face and slam them into oblivion. I *wanted* to do less. I had given myself *permission* to do less. The old rules just needed to GO THE *F* AWAY.

After struggling against these rules for a few weeks, I sat down on my patio and journaled about the conflict. As what often happens when I write, an epiphany rose out of the ethers: Instead of *fighting*, I needed to *surrender*.

Judgment wasn't the answer. Beating the old rules to a pulp wasn't the way to go, no matter how much I wanted to destroy them. Instead, I needed to surrender to what felt good. I needed to follow pleasure and slowness. I needed to attend to what my spirit desired.

Immediate relief loosened my body when I had this epiphany. I felt a weight lift. My shoulders dropped. I sunk into my chair, looked out at the courtyard of grass and trees in front of my patio, and took a breath.

Finally. I had space.

The guilt went away. The discomfort melted. I was *free*.

Magical things started to happen as I surrendered into the space I had created. All the work I'd done through my recent break came together. I didn't just *know* I was worthy, desirable, and whole—I *believed* it. I went on dates and actually enjoyed them—an entirely new experience for me! I had nothing to prove to my date. I didn't have to convince him to be interested in me. I didn't need to amp myself up to impress or shrink myself down to conform. I just got to be me, finally free from the shame that had strangled my spirit for so long.

The magic also showed up in my creativity. Before giving myself this space, I knew something was hovering inside me. It felt like a new book was rumbling up and wanting to be written. I had been collecting notes and ideas on these rumblings for months, but I didn't know what it all was. I certainly didn't have a name for it.

Then, one day as I sat on my patio reading *Women Who Run with the Wolves*, the phrase "grounded wildness" came to me. I immediately stopped reading, grabbed my journal, and captured the torrent of ideas gushing forward. Without even having to decide, I knew that "grounded wildness" was it. That would be the title of this book.

Even more importantly, I *felt* grounded wildness. I was *living* in grounded wildness. These two words perfectly captured the newfound freedom I had discovered through my breaks. I was simultaneously rooted to the earth and dancing in the wind. Soaring in the air while tethered to my core. Completely undone and more whole than I'd ever felt. I was free.

This is what happens when you have space. Ideas emerge. *You* emerge.

Space is about reconnecting with yourself. It's about letting your mind wander and hearing yourself think. It's about having the room to feel yourself in your body. It's about noticing how a warm wind feels on your face and the juicy ecstasy of a perfectly ripe summer tomato. It's about being present, knowing you are allowed to be right where you are without having to jump on the next item on your to-do list. It's about stopping and simply being there with yourself.

Does that sound wonderful? And a little terrifying? If so, you're not alone. We do so much numbing to remove ourselves from ourselves. We binge on food and wine, and watch Netflix for hours. We scroll endlessly on social media. We cram our schedules so full that there's no time to feel.

We numb ourselves because having space is often uncomfortable—at least initially. You feel guilty for taking the time for yourself. Rules jump in; and the inner critic starts scolding you, saying that you should do more, get all the things done for work, call your sister, check in on your dad, respond to the email your kid's teacher sent yesterday, do some yoga, get dinner going, or whatever "shoulds" your inner critic enjoys prescribing to you.

This discomfort can go beyond guilt for breaking the rules, though. When you have space, emotions you don't particularly want to feel may arise. Questions you've been trying to avoid may come forward. Sitting with your truth can be unsettling, even if that unsettledness can lead you to greater freedom.

A big part of grounded wildness comes from getting comfortable with being with yourself. You have to stop performing for yourself before you can stop performing for others. You require space to listen to the truth about who you are. It's the gateway to feeling your feelings, connecting to your aliveness, following your knowing, claiming yourself, and doing every other practice in this book.

Creating space also makes it easier to disconnect from all the voices shouting the rules into your ears and urging you to perform. It allows you to sink into yourself and let go of the pressure to prove, please, and perfect.

Pausing reminds you that all the tenets of grounded wildness
are true. You are whole, worthy, and complete. You belong
within. You are radiant. No performing is needed.

Finally, space creates the capacity to consider new possibilities in your life. I loved most of my jobs at the first
company I worked for after grad school, but it was *busy*.
I didn't know how to set boundaries, and the company culture
didn't set them for me, either. I regularly caught up on email
in the evenings. Sick days simply meant working from home
and attempting to sneak in a nap between meetings. There
was always more work than I could come close to finishing.

After eight years there, I moved companies. On my
new team, people typically got to work between 8:00
and 8:30 a.m.—and they were GONE by 5:00 p.m. Many
of them took a midday break to do a quick shopping trip
to Target, walk the skyways, or meet a friend for lunch.
People stayed home and *didn't work* when they were sick.
I can count on two hands the number of times I worked
a night or weekend in my two and a half years there. I worked
hard and had plenty to do, but my plate wasn't overflowing.
I was just at capacity. This was a totally foreign concept to me.

For the first time in years, I had the time and energy
to explore. I signed up for community ed writing classes.
I volunteered every week for an entire summer with Latinx
preschoolers while their parents took English classes. I joined
my first nonprofit board. I slept more.

When my job changed at that company to something
I knew I wouldn't like, I had the capacity to consider different
options in my life. Sure, I could go find another corporate job.

But maybe there was another possibility. Maybe I could start a business. Maybe, just maybe, there was another way to work and live than what I had previously considered.

I had the chance to take a different direction because I had the space to dream up different visions for my life. I had the energy to consider big questions about what I wanted from work, the impact I hoped to create, and where I was being called. My inner voice had space to let itself be known, which gave me the clarity to follow it regardless of what other people thought or whether it made sense on paper. Space allowed me to see a new path and believe it was possible to start walking down it.

Even though I was nowhere near living in grounded wildness, leaving my corporate job to start a business was the act of a grounded, wild woman. While I had never followed the perfect path of expectations in my career, this was the first time since starting corporate work that I embraced the risk of a hard left off the path. Even though I jumped right back into performing the second I started my business, the exploration I went through to leave my corporate job was a pause from performing. I got off the hamster wheel, took a breath, and listened to what my life was telling me.

Space allowed for a new chapter of my life to emerge.

Creating Your Own Space

I purposefully titled this chapter "Create Space." I know as well as you do that space is not going to magically land in your lap. The world will pile more and more on top of you.

The rules will tell you to take it all on. They will command you to give all your energy to others while you wither on the vine.

I hope our culture is changing. I hope the corset of overdoing is loosening. At the same time, you can't wait for culture to change to get the space you need (or anything else you want, for that matter!). To get space, you must design your life for it—and then give yourself permission to take it.

Yes, you are going against the grain by creating space in your life. Yes, it will mean you have to say no to someone—or probably several someones. You will likely get pushback. You may feel guilty. This is all true.

It's also worth it. Space clears the path to your freedom.

So how do you do it? How do you create space in the midst of a culture that would prefer to squeeze every drop of everything out of you?

Let's start small. Here are several ideas:

- Lie on the floor for ten minutes and do nothing. Don't worry about meditating, napping, or doing anything specific. Just lie there.
- Take a walk without your phone. If you must have your phone, tuck it in your pocket and don't use it for anything.
- Drive without listening to the radio.
- Watch a sunset.
- Say no to one thing you would have typically said yes to, then block that time to do something that feels good.
- Take a nap.

- Journal for five minutes.
- Take a solo lunch break and eat outside in the sun.
- Get to your child's daycare fifteen minutes before you need to pick them up, then sit in your car and close your eyes. I had a coaching client who did this, and she loved it!

You'll probably notice a theme to these suggestions. In every single one, you are *alone* and *quiet*. You're not scrolling through your phone, paying attention to a podcast, or even listening to music. You are taking away the numbing devices that distract you from yourself so that you can listen to what you know is true. So that you can hear the rumblings of your grounded wildness.

Creating space in small ways is both approachable and helpful. Overhauling your entire schedule can feel overwhelming and downright impossible. But ten minutes? You can find ten minutes.

Sometimes, though, more space is needed. If you feel that need, listen. Do what you can to fulfill it. Challenge the voices saying you can't, and look for possibilities. Here are a few ways I've seen people create more space in their lives:

- Change jobs to a role that requires fewer hours for a company that has greater respect for work-life balance.
- Leave your partner and kids at home and take a vacation *by yourself*. This may seem impossible, but I just met a woman who did this. She has ten- and twelve-year-old boys at home. And she's a teacher.

And she took NINE DAYS all to herself.

- Sign up to work with a coach or therapist for a few months. This is an especially helpful approach if it's difficult for you to create space entirely on your own, but you respond well to the accountability of investing money in yourself or having an appointment on your calendar.

- Go to a meditation class, church prayer group, full moon circle, intuitive movement class, or any other program that creates a structured space for you to get in touch with yourself. I regularly do activities like this, and they have been so helpful. Plus, it's fun to say you're going to a full moon circle!

- Take a critical look at all your commitments and decide what needs to go. Examine everything from your book club to church to volunteering. Start by cutting the activities you find the least fulfilling. Even if you're afraid of hurting the feelings of the gourmet dinner group you've been a part of for ten years but you don't really enjoy anymore, it's worth eliminating it from your schedule. I know it isn't easy, but I promise you will survive.

- Take a second, critical look at what you're committed to on other people's behalf, like your kids or an elderly parent. When I was about twelve, my parents told me and my brother that we weren't going to do traveling sports and out-of-town tennis tournaments because they didn't want to spend their weekends on the road. Even at the time, I thought this made sense. As I've gotten older, I've appreciated their example more, even though I don't have kids of my own. Their lives were not supposed to revolve completely around me and my brother. You get to have your own life too.

Now, choose something for yourself. Ask what kind of space you need and challenge yourself to make it possible. Start small *or* big. Listen to yourself. Follow your needs and desires.

You're already moving toward grounded wildness.

CHAPTER 14

Feel Your Feelings

have historically been pretty bad at feeling my feelings. Instead of allowing my feelings to arise and flow through me, I tended to ignore them, shove them down, put on a happy face, and get on with things—until the inevitable moment came when the feelings would be so built up that they had nowhere to go but out. They usually exploded as a gushing waterfall of tears. Occasionally, they'd come out as a snide remark or unprovoked anger, but usually they left as tears. Most of the time I would cry alone, not wanting to show those big feelings to anyone.

Over the past decade, I've gradually learned how to feel my feelings. First on my own, slowing down long enough to notice and feel my emotions. Later, I learned to feel my feelings in front of trusted people.

There's no way around it: Feeling your feelings is vulnerable. It's also *freeing*. There's liberation in accepting whatever you're feeling without judgment, without cramming it down or throwing it away, and without making it bigger or smaller than it actually is. The poem "Stay Awake," which you read in chapter 4, says it directly:

> Find freedom in allowing your feelings to flow,
> Nothing held back, you can let it all show.

Burying your feelings does the opposite. Ignoring hard emotions like grief, disappointment, and rage takes you away from your truth. Holding back joy, wonder, and serenity dims your light. Avoiding both sides of the spectrum dulls your aliveness. It severs your grounding and tamps down the wild woman inside.

Feeling your feelings is a gateway back to you—and a gateway to grounded wildness. You cannot go through big breaks without feeling. In fact, the core of breaking down *is* feeling. It's about allowing all your emotions to arise and being there with them.

Looking back, I believe this is one of the reasons my final break (or maybe I should say "my most recent break," as I'm sure there will be others!) was so massive—and why my emotions felt disproportionately large to the situation at hand. After minimizing my reactions for so long, I *finally* gave myself permission to come undone and feel all the emotions I'd been carrying for thirty years. Allowing myself to completely break down was the first step toward breaking open and rediscovering my freedom.

There are two practices that have allowed me to feel my feelings and use them as a guide to grounded wildness. Before we delve into those practices, however, we need to address the barriers that get in the way of feeling your feelings. Yes, it is vulnerable. But the rules that are holding you back go deeper than simple human vulnerability.

These rules knock you down for experiencing certain emotions in the first place—and then knock you down again for having the nerve to express them. Everyone has different emotional rules passed down to them, and there's no way I could possibly list them all. So instead, I'm going to highlight the most common rules I've seen that stand in the way of feeling your feelings.

Rule #1: "I Should Just Be Grateful"

I've heard so many women say these exact words when they're feeling called toward a change in their lives. Let me be clear: Gratitude is wonderful. The positive benefits of practicing gratitude are researched and real. So please, recognize all you have. Be grateful for your home, job, salary, health, and all the fantastic people in your life.

Gratitude, however, is not a cover for other emotions. It's not a guilt trip for how you think you *should* be feeling. You can be grateful for your job *and* disappointed you didn't get the new role you wanted. You can be grateful for your salary *and* angry it's not on par with your male colleagues. You can be grateful for your entire life *and* know there's something different out there for you.

You can be grateful *and* feel any other emotion at the same time.

This isn't the message many have gotten, though. Instead of being taught to accept the full range of your emotions, you may have been handed the message that gratitude should overpower everything. You may have been coached to deny yourself what you truly desire in the name of being grateful for what you already have. Not only does this keep your more "challenging" emotions in check, but it also keeps you unquestioning and undemanding. This rule maintains the status quo—for you as an individual, and for all of us collectively.

You deserve more than *only* being grateful. Your grounded wildness will demand it.

Rule #2: "I Shouldn't Be Too Much"

Ugh. Don't even get me started on this one. I hear it from women ALL THE TIME. Maybe you've been told it directly ("You're a little much," "You're kind of a lot," etc.). Maybe it's been communicated to you more indirectly, like through an eye roll or a look that reads *Here we go again* when you open your mouth to share your opinion.

You can see how this quickly translates into causing you to hold back your feelings, especially the big ones that might make other people uncomfortable. If you've started to tear up at work and received an exasperated look or a judgmental question like "Are you CRYING?" then you've gotten the message that your emotions are too much for the work-place. If someone asks how you are and you share a deep disappointment you just experienced only to be told to "look on the bright side," you get the message that "I'm fine" will be the appropriate response next time. If you shake and sob after a deep grief and people literally leave the room, you learn that shaking and sobbing are best left as pri-vate activities.

This also goes for emotions on the other side of the spectrum. Unadulterated joy is at least as big as grief or anger—and it can make some people just as uncomfort-able. Several years ago, I was dancing without any inhibitions at a friend's wedding. I was loving life, flailing my arms in the air, twirling in circles, and shimmying my way across the dance floor without a care in the world. I wasn't giving a second thought to how I looked or who might be watch-ing—until I got off the dance floor, and another friend looked at me and said, "You were dancing BIG." Like the guy I dated who told me I didn't need any caffeine, she didn't mean it as a compliment.

In a split second, my joy was squashed. I simultaneously wanted to sit out the rest of the night *and* get back out there and dance even bigger, just to show her. I probably responded somewhere between those two—not completely hiding myself, but not fully displaying my joy, either.

This doesn't mean you get to dump your emotions on everyone around you. But you also don't need to con-strict your feelings into a tidy box to make other people comfortable. You don't need to mute your colors or subdue the fullness of your own experience. People will eventually get used to seeing a woman living in her fullness.

Or not. Either way, it's not your responsibility.

You can never be too much. Or too little. You just are.

Rule #3: "Nice Girls Don't Get Angry"

This rule is an extension of "I shouldn't be too much," but it runs so deep that it deserves its own category.

Many women have been advised that their anger is unacceptable. If you've ever expressed displeasure and been told to just "smile a little more, honey," then you've gotten this message loud and clear.

This is especially true for Black women, who are often given direct feedback that they are angry and making other people uncomfortable with their anger. They are told in clear terms that their emotions are threatening. White women are often the ones precipitating this feedback, whether they are giving it directly to the individual or talking to their manager or HR, who then passes this "feedback" along.

One thing is right about what Black women are being told: Anger is a threat. But unless the situation is violent or abusive, anger is not a personal threat. Rather, *it's a threat to the entire system.* Anger spurs action. Women who feel and express their anger from a place of grounded wildness are going to change the world.

Rule #4: "I Have to Stay in Control"

Take a deep breath for this one. For some people, part of feeling like you have to stay in control is related to the rules about being too much and getting angry. You force your-self to stay in control because of the feedback you've gotten and the discomfort you've seen on other people's faces when you let all your feelings show. Or, you may *need* to stay in control to keep yourself safe in a turbulent situation.

That can all be true, but that's not what I'm talking about here. Instead, I'm talking about the discomfort YOU feel when you lose control and allow your emotions to run free, even when you're sitting alone in your house with no possibility of anyone else seeing your emotions.

During my years of performing and shoving down my feelings, it wasn't that I was unemotional. Instead, the opposite was true. I felt my emotions so deeply that I didn't know what to do with them. They felt too big, too all-encompassing, too profound—too EVERYTHING. I didn't know how to be deeply sad and just be with that sadness. I didn't know how to sit with any hard emotion and let it be there.

So I put the lid on my feelings. I numbed. I overworked, overate, and overexercised. I went back to my to-do list when emotions came up. I cried when the emotions were so full that I didn't have any choice but to cry and release them. I got uncomfortable when those tears became a little too big or when I felt the emotions a little too deeply. I didn't know what would happen if I truly lost control and let myself feel everything I was feeling.

I found out during my second big break. Of course, I had felt big emotions before that part of my life. I had experienced grief, disappointment, rejection, fear, shame, joy, and wonder, but none of them felt as intense as what came up during the break. For several days, my emotions felt bottomless, like there was some volcano buried deep in my belly that just kept erupting. Every time I thought the torrent of lava had subsided, another eruption came blasting out of nowhere.

I had completely and totally lost control. I hated it. But it was exactly what I needed.

That volcano of emotion was a path back to me. It caused me to ask deep questions. It made me uncover the rules that had buried parts of me for so many years. The pain didn't eat me up and swallow me whole. Instead, it broke down all the barriers between me and my radiance. Between me and my worthiness. Between me and my grounded wildness.

Losing control was the path back to being found. It can do the same for you. *

Rule #5: "I Shouldn't Be a Burden"

It was late March 2020, just a few weeks into the pandemic. Stay-at-home orders were in place across the US and much of the world. No one knew what was going to happen, how long it would last, or just how bad COVID-19 would get. It felt like the entire world had been tossed into an avalanche with no sense of direction. The uncertainty of the moment was absolutely overwhelming.

---

* I said it earlier in this book, and I'm going to say it again: If your emotions ever feel like too much, reach out to a therapist, counselor, doctor, etc. for further support.

And I was living alone.

One day in late March, I went for a walk outside. As I hiked along, people moved their bodies away from mine as we passed on opposite sides of a ten-foot-wide path. They inched to the edge of the trail and tilted their bodies as far away from me as possible without actually falling down. Rationally, I got it. But every angled body felt like a personal rejection.

What's more, it felt like everyone I encountered was with someone else. Couples were walking hand in hand. Families of all ages were strolling together. Then there was me. Alone.

At some point during the walk, a little dog scurried in my direction. I found myself drawn to the dog, wanting it to come closer so I could pet it. Instead, it sauntered right past me. I was filled with disappointment, despite the fact that I'm not a huge dog person. I realized in that moment that I hadn't touched another living thing in over two weeks.

Later that evening, I read an article in *The Atlantic* that provided several different scenarios for how the pandemic could shake out. None of them were good. Studying the possibilities plunged me deep into knowing it would likely be many more weeks before I would touch another living thing.

That was when the despair hit. I cried. A LOT. I attempted to go to bed and sleep it off, but I just lay there awake, tears soaking my pillow. So I got up and started to write. I wrote exactly what I was feeling in the middle of feeling it. It was raw, unencumbered, and the complete and total truth.

I knew it had to be shared.

There was just one problem: I didn't want people to worry about me. I didn't want to make other people feel sad by reading about my sadness. I didn't want to burden anyone with my big emotions.

Yet I knew it had to be shared. I knew that communicating the truth would create connection and show people that they weren't alone in their emotions, even if they were physically alone at home.

On that day, in that moment, the desire to share my truth and create connection outweighed my fear of being a burden. So I put my words into a blog post and titled it "Living Along During a Pandemic." Then I shared it on LinkedIn and my personal Facebook page.

Both my fears and my desires came true. Heaps of people commented on the post and sent me thank-you messages saying that they felt exactly the same way. Friends offered to have me quarantine with them (as long as I brought my own toilet paper!).

It made other people feel sad. While I didn't enjoy that, it was okay. I realized I could no longer hold back my truth because of the concern that it might make someone sad. Or that they might worry about me. Or that they might be disappointed in me.

I've come up against this rule many times since posting "Living Alone During a Pandemic." I feel it every time I share something hard. It's come up on several occasions as I think about people reading this book. I've had to remind those in my life that they need to remember the joyful stories I share as well, because they are just as much the truth as the grief and anxiety are.

I don't share everything. Far from it. But I can't pretend to be happy all the time to keep other people comfortable. I refuse to hide away challenging emotions to protect people from my feelings. I can no longer bury myself in an attempt to not be a burden.

Rule #6: "It's Not Safe to Show My Feelings"

This is the final rule I want to discuss briefly before moving into the practices to feel your feelings. It isn't my area of expertise, so I want to be careful. I also know it's not safe for everyone to express their true emotions, and it would be irresponsible of me to ignore that.

For example, if showing your emotions as a kid got you physically or emotionally hurt, then hiding, numbing, and ignoring your feelings may have become a survival mechanism. It may still be a survival mechanism in some of your relationships. If you work in a culture where displaying your feelings results in people insisting that you're angry or sensitive and you getting overlooked for opportunities, then you might hold back your feelings to avoid those consequences.

I hope you can get out of the current situations that are forcing you to mask yourself or get help to work through past traumas. I also want you to know you're doing the best you can right now.

How to Practice Feeling Your Feelings

No matter what rules and barriers we face, nearly all of us need to practice feeling our feelings. Here are two tools that have helped me go from an emotional shover-downer to more of an emotional flow state. The first is a pathway through any emotion you are experiencing, regardless of the size of that feeling or where it falls on the spectrum of serenity and joy to rage and grief. The second practice goes a layer deeper and utilizes your emotions as an avenue to self-discovery and aliveness.

Practice #1: Three Steps to Feeling Your Feelings

In 2012, I received an offer to move to Australia for a year to fill in for a colleague on maternity leave. I jumped at the opportunity and said yes, with total conviction and commitment.

At the time the offer came in, I was working on a temporary assignment in Virginia for three months. Once the Australia offer was finalized, I packed up my Honda Civic and drove home to be in Minnesota for a month before getting on a plane to fly 10,000 miles around the globe to Melbourne.

Those few weeks in Minnesota were total chaos. I attempted to visit every human in my life who I'd already gone three months without seeing. I sifted through my belongings to determine what I would need during my year Down Under, then packed up everything else so that my condo could be rented while I was gone. I got my visas, medical appointments, flights, and all other paperwork in order. All the while, I was still working for the job in Virginia remotely.

As you might imagine, there were just a few emotions floating around during this time.

On the one hand, I was happy, grateful, and excited. I loved working globally and craved adventure. I couldn't wait to see what the year would bring!

On the other hand, I was overwhelmed, nervous, scared, and sad. I didn't let myself feel any of those feelings.

I thought I was only allowed to be excited, grateful, and happy. On top of that, I didn't have time to feel my feelings! There were a million things I had to get done. So I shoved those feelings down whenever they arose and got back to my to-do list.

Until one day, when I got on the phone with a life coach and proceeded to cry for an entire hour. All the feelings I'd been attempting to bury surged to the surface, finally overwhelming my ability to ignore and control them.

My coach listened as I cried. She held space for everything I was feeling. She asked questions and listened some more. Then, together, we came up with a plan for feeling my feelings. It's a three-step process I've been using ever since and shared during countless speaking engagements:

1. Give yourself permission to stop and feel.
2. Name what you're feeling *without judgment*.
3. Sit with the emotion and *feel* it.

Let's dive into each of these steps further.

Step #1: Give Yourself Permission to Stop and Feel

It's unlikely you'll find this step if you Google how to feel your feelings, but I think it's the most important. If you don't give yourself permission to stop and create space to feel, you can't do any of the other steps.

I know you can't always stop and feel everything in the moment you are feeling it. While I desire a world where we can be our full human selves all the time, I understand you might not feel comfortable (or be allowed) to break down in the middle of a meeting. You might not trust your colleagues enough to show all of who you are all the time. This doesn't just go for work. It might be true with certain friends or family members as well. While I hope you have some places where you are allowed to be totally free (more on that in chapter 21), I know this won't be true every day in every place.

In those situations, simply come back to your feelings. I promise, they will still be there! Create space later in the day or week and then give yourself permission to stop and feel. Once you're there, move on to step two.

Step #2: Name What You're Feeling Without Judgment

Have you heard the phrase, "Name it to tame it?" That's what this is. After you stop and give yourself permission, name what you are feeling. Literally. Say out loud, "I feel disappointed right now," or "I'm feeling grief right now."

Most of us aren't taught how to recognize our emotions. So if you're coming up empty when you try to name the exact feeling you're experiencing, describe how the emotion feels in your body instead. For example, "I feel like someone is sitting on my chest. The weight is creeping around my heart and squeezing it." Or, "I feel a huge pit in my stomach. Like a boulder, just sitting there. It's so big, it's almost making me nauseous."

Now comes the "without judgment" piece. There is no "should" when it comes to your emotions. They aren't good or bad, right or wrong. Whatever you're feeling is just what you're feeling. That's it.

If you're experiencing guilt or shame over the emotions you're feeling, then name that, too! For instance, "I'm feeling sad. I'm also feeling guilty that I'm sad when so many people have it worse off than me. I feel like I should be grateful, not sad." The shoulds and shouldn'ts that arise in response to your feelings are usually connected to the rules you've been taught. Naming and noticing them will start the process of breaking down those rules, letting go of performing, and moving toward grounded wildness.

Step #3: Sit with the Emotion and Feel It

This is usually the hardest part. I mean, if you haven't even been taught how to name what you're feeling, how are you supposed to just sit there and be with it?!

Yet that's exactly what you need to do. Lean into the discomfort and allow yourself to feel whatever it is you're feeling. Notice what's happening in your body. Get curious about everything you're experiencing. Be with it. Be with yourself.

Sometimes sitting with your emotions is quite literal. In the busy days after creating this three-step process and before moving to Australia, I would notice a feeling coming up as I rushed around trying to get everything done. Instead of ignoring it (like I had done previously), I would stop, sit down, take a breath, and say out loud, "I am over-whelmed right now." Then I would sit there and feel it. Usually, the sense of overwhelm would dissipate in a minute or two, and then I could return to my to-do list with a calmer heart and a greater sense of space inside me.

Other times, sitting with your emotions isn't sitting at all. Instead, you need to move through your emotions by dancing, running, lying on the floor as you cry and beat your hands on the ground, kickboxing, walking—or whatever feels good to you. This isn't about numbing or trying to force out the emotions quickly. Instead, you are aligning your body with the emotion, allowing yourself to feel it through your movements, and eventually releasing it.

Practice #2: Use Your Feelings as a Guide Back to You

Your feelings are a map back into yourself. They light the path toward what you desire and long for. They inspire you and anger you to take action toward the changes you want to see in the world. They hold up a candle to what is most important to you—and if you listen, they prompt you to keep exploring those values.

Using your feelings as a guide back to you comes down to one very simple question: What is this feeling telling me?

When I went through my second break, my feelings told me that there was A LOT happening—way more than just the immediate situation. My feelings let me know that I needed help to sort and sift through everything that was coming up and change my story once and for all. They guided me to reach out to a therapist, and that action changed my life.

Feelings have also guided me in day-to-day ways that don't require a complete breakdown. Envy has given me clues about what I desire. Regret has shown me where I want to make changes going forward. Fulfillment and flow have shone a flashlight on how to spend my time and energy. Wonder has guided me to greater connection with the larger world, both physically and spiritually. Small situations that trigger big feelings have illuminated where I need to further explore and heal.

None of the feelings I listed (nor any others I didn't list) are positive or negative. They're just information. They're a GPS into yourself, through your breaks, and into grounded wildness.

So when emotions arise, ask yourself, "What is this feeling telling me?" Depending on how you're feeling, this question may look like the following:

- What is this anger telling me?
- What is this joy telling me?
- What is this frustration telling me?
- What is this grief telling me?
- What is this pride telling me?

You can also connect your feelings to the sensations you are experiencing in your body, whether you can name the specific emotion or not. Here are a few examples:

- What is this light, bubbly feeling in my chest telling me?

- What is the pit in my stomach telling me?
- What is the grounded relaxation in my pelvis telling me?

You can journal your answers to these questions, meditate on them, or simply pause and ask yourself in the moment and see what arises.

Then sit with the responses. The answers may be enlightening, fulfilling, or significantly uncomfortable. Maybe all three at once! Continue to be there with your feelings. Practice curiosity and compassion. Feel your way through the temptation to go back to performing. Sink, swallow, and let your truth thrive. This is where you are most alive.

CHAPTER 15

Follow Aliveness

When I started my business, I coached a lot of women in career transitions. Most of them knew they needed a change but were unsure of their next steps. They wanted to be purposeful—and they needed help figuring out what was right for them.

As part of the coaching, I conducted a strengths interview with each woman. I always started by asking fairly typical questions like, "Tell me about a time you were successful and had a big impact. What did you do to make it a success?" and "What are you doing when people are blown away by you?"

In response to these questions, the women would give me typical answers about projects at work and feedback they'd received from previous managers. It was all accurate and true—and usually a little rote, like it had been rehearsed before.

Then I would ask a different question: "When are you most *alive*?"

Inevitably, something completely different would come out of their mouths than anything they had mentioned earlier in the interview. It was like a part of *them* had come alive simply by answering the question.

My interview with Chloe sticks out in particular. Prior to this coaching session, I would have described Chloe as reserved, creative, and analytical. Little did I know that a different kind of woman was lurking just below the surface.

When I asked Chloe when she felt most alive, she immediately launched into a story: "Well, this one time, I was at a demolition derby . . ."

Demolition derby?! I thought. I NEVER would have pictured Chloe at a demolition derby!

"And they had a drawing for people to drive one of the demolition cars," she continued. "So I put my name in—and they drew it! I got to drive one of the cars with the real demolition derby drivers—and I won second place! It was so awesome! I definitely felt alive then."

My inner monologue continued, *Driving a demolition car?! What?! Who is this woman?!*

She wasn't finished, though. "Also, when I ride my mountain bike, I feel super alive then. And this one time, I was part of a drum circle. I could feel the rhythm in every part of me, and it made me feel *alive*."

My jaw continued to drop with every example she shared. This woman wasn't reserved! She was a demolition-derby-driving, mountain-bike-riding, drum-circling BADASS! She just didn't allow her aliveness to come to the surface very often. Instead, she tucked her badass self away much of the time in favor of a cocoon of stability and comfort.

Part of her was more comfortable in the cocoon. The badass was a risk-taker. She followed her intuition and didn't worry about what other people thought of her. That was scary.

By the time Chloe and I started working together, she was ready for deep change. This was more than just career coaching, and we both knew it. Chloe had been persisting in her cocoon so long that she had outgrown it.

The cocoon had been fine for many years. I think Chloe would say she even needed that cocoon at one point in her life. But she didn't need it anymore.

Chloe's desire to be alive was stronger than any of her fears. The risk of staying in the cocoon was far greater than the risk of emerging and living as her full, alive, badass self. "Fine" was no longer enough.

She was ready to get grounded and wild.

What Is Aliveness?

I live near an open space with great hiking trails in the foothills of Colorado. The paths at this open space traverse through high, rolling prairies; scrubby bushes; cactus (which erupt in gorgeous blooms in the spring!); wildflowers; flowing grass; and the occasional pine tree. The whole area emanates openness and freedom. It's a place where I can take a deep breath.

At one point along the trail, a short "social" (i.e., unofficial) path leads off the main thoroughfare toward a set of flat rocks along a ledge several hundred feet high. To the east, the prairie stretches as far as the eye can see. To the south, the Flatirons rise out of Boulder. To the west, Longs Peak looms against several smaller summits rising out of Rocky Mountain National Park.

I call this place my Lion King Rocks, because it feels just like the ridge where Rafiki lifted baby Simba to present him to all the animals. Only, this is a little higher. And with prairie dogs scampering around below instead of giraffes.

I feel alive most of the time I'm out hiking, but here on my Lion King Rocks, it's a guarantee. I breathe the expansive landscape deep into my soul. I am simultaneously connected to it all and a separate individual. Every fiber of my being is activated, yet I am totally calm.

I don't worry about what I need to get done or whether I'm behind where I "should" be in my business. I'm not attached to what other people may be thinking about me. I'm not trying to control anything. The rules melt away. There are no shoulds and supposed-tos. I have nothing to prove. Nothing to perform. I'm just ALIVE.

Aliveness is life force. It is you, awake. It's how you go from simply surviving to truly *thriving*. It's a path to reclaim your radiance. Rediscovering your aliveness is rediscovering YOU.

Aliveness is not about having to be high-energy, ecstatic, and blowing the lid off life all the time. It *can* be that, but it doesn't *have* to be. Aliveness can be dancing with total abandon or summiting a 14,000-foot peak. It can also be a deep conversation with a friend or sitting quietly in the grass, feeling the earth beneath you. It can be experiencing joy, wonder, awe, serenity, grief, disappointment, rage—and the breadth and depth of any other emotion within you. It's about being present to the full experience of life.

Following aliveness has been a path back to my radiant self, just like it was a path for Chloe to rediscover her badassery. Following your aliveness may be as simple as noticing what makes you come alive and doing that. Done, and done. If that works for you, there's no need to overcomplicate things. However, I know it can be helpful to put more structure around aliveness to give you ideas for where to notice and pursue it in your own life. I like to think of following aliveness in three ways:

1. Seeking out aliveness
2. Turning yourself on to the aliveness that's already present
3. Using aliveness as a guide for your life as a whole

Seek Out Aliveness

I'm seeking out aliveness when I put my feet into the dirt on a hiking trail or when I sit on my Lion King Rocks. I'm seeking out aliveness when I reach out to a friend who allows me to be full, real, and authentic without any effort at all. I'm seeking out aliveness when I travel to a new country, go on a mini-adventure around Colorado, dance, listen to live music, play my guitar, and sing.

When I'm feeling disconnected from myself, sucked back into the rules, or just plain blah, any of these activities will prompt me to come back alive—usually almost immediately. It's amazing how fast it works.

I call this the Aliveness Agenda. It's your personal list of people, places, and activities that put you in a position to reconnect with your aliveness. They clear out the crud standing in the way of your fire and ignite a spark of grounded wildness inside you.

My Aliveness Agenda is listed in the first paragraph. Yours may be completely different. There's no right or wrong; there is only what works for you. If you aren't sure what's on your list, use these reflection questions to help you brainstorm.

- **People:** Who do you feel alive around? Who accepts you and encourages you to be exactly who you are, with no proving, pleasing, performing, or rebelling needed? Your people may be individuals, groups, or an entire community, like a church.
- **Places:** What environments feel most like you? Where do you feel most at home?
- **Activities:** What activities bring you joy and flow? What are you doing when you lose track of time? What reconnects you to you?

Or you can just ask one overarching question: *When do you feel both grounded and wild?* THAT is your Aliveness Agenda.

Turn Yourself On

Yep. You read that one correctly. It's time to turn yourself on. I don't necessarily mean sexually, although that can be part of it. Instead, I mean turning yourself on to the aliveness that already exists at any given moment, no matter where you are, what you're doing, who you are with, or if you're alone.

I first heard of this concept of turning yourself on from world-renowned psychotherapist Esther Perel. I immediately loved it. Turning yourself on is a different kind of eroticism, one that spans way beyond the bounds of sexuality. It's about creating the space to notice, and then bring forth, the life force running beneath the surface. You don't have to create any-thing—you just have to notice the charge that's already there.

Every summer throughout middle and high school, I would go with a huge group of friends to a cabin in northern Minnesota for a long weekend. We'd cram into bunk beds; set up tents for those who couldn't fit inside; and spend the weekend swimming, boating, pulling pranks, and generally playing. It was all high-energy. We barely slept. It was awesome.

One summer, there was a quiet, gray day that wasn't particularly conducive to any of our normal cabin activ-ities. The speed boat stayed tied to the dock, and everyone piled into the cabin to slowly chat the day away.

Another force was calling me, however. Instead of staying inside with everyone else, I decided to take a kayak out alone.

The lake was like glass. Thick clouds hung low, pulling a blanket over the entire region. My kayak was the only thing breaking the stillness. Even the loons seemed to have decided it was a good day for a nap. I paddled as quietly as humanly possible, not wanting to upset the deep calm.

At one point, I stopped paddling and paused in the middle of the lake. Holding onto the paddle with my left hand, I gently dipped the fingers of my right hand into the water and then pulled them out, feeling every drop of water glide down my hand and drip back into the lake. I dipped my fingers into the lake again, this time swirling them around and noticing the patterns they made. I sensed how the water moved around my fingers as I caressed the lake.

In that moment, I was connected to myself, the lake, and the entire natural world around me. I felt the water in a visceral, sensual way, quite literally using my senses to notice it all. I was present to exactly where I was and what I was doing, in both a physical sense and in a spiritual way. I was TURNED ON.

There was nothing fancy about this experience. I didn't get on a plane and travel halfway around the world. I didn't throw a party or organize a fun event. I didn't concoct anything at all. I just followed my desire to kayak and became present to the aliveness that was already there.

Aliveness exists in the wind on your face, the scent of lilacs in the spring, and the melding colors of a sunset. Aliveness lives in the sweet, juicy crunch of tomato-peach bruschetta as it hits your tongue and the warm bitterness of a great cup of coffee as it slides down your throat. It's communicated through music, laughter, and the way someone catches your eye and smiles.

Aliveness is present in every moment. You just have

to notice it—which requires space.

It's hard to notice aliveness when you're trying to do a million things at once. So go back to the ideas for creating space listed in chapter 13 and see what aliveness you detect when you slow down.

You can also do a purposeful practice of noticing aliveness. Go to the nearest flower. (It may be in a vase, your yard, or a public garden.) Bend down and smell that flower, allowing its essence to waft through your nostrils into your very being. Don't quit there. Reach out and touch the petals, feeling their softness between your fingertips. Notice the brilliant colors of the flower and the deep green of the stem. Take a breath, and allow it all to sink in. How does your body feel?

You may notice yourself getting a little turned on just by reading that paragraph! This is further proof that aliveness is everywhere. You don't even have to be with the flower to feel alive. You just have to read about the flower, and it ignites something inside you.

So go ahead. Turn yourself on.

Use Aliveness as a Guide

So far in this chapter, we've talked about seeking out aliveness and noticing it in small, day-to-day moments. These are wonderful practices to continually reconnect to your grounded wildness. You can, however, also use aliveness as a guide for your entire life.

We often notice when things are bad, like when you get a pit in your stomach on Sunday night as you think about going to work on Monday morning. Or when a relationship is full of tension and strife. Or when your body breaks down and you get sick.

It's great to notice when things are bad. Those situations can be fantastic motivators for change. Taking action based only on bad circumstances is incomplete, however. You never want to only move *away* from what is bad. You also want to move *toward* what makes you feel alive.

The initial push for me to quit my corporate job was the bad. My job had changed from something I loved to something I immediately knew I would hate. I had to fight back tears in my boss's office when I got the news (which also happened on my birthday—talk about a sign from the Universe!). No one knew how I was feeling. I put on a smiling face and performed my way through the new job, as all the rules told me to do. But inside, I knew something had to shift—and fast. Every fiber of my being screamed at me to make a change.

At first, the energy motivating me was simple: "Get me out of here!" As I started to explore possible next steps, however, the energy started to shift. As I reflected on what I really desired in my career and life and talked to other entrepreneurs, ideas started flowing for a possible business. My creativity shot off the charts. I thought of workshops I could host, books I could write, and people I could coach. I got *excited*.

I felt engaged in a way I had never known in my corporate career. My brain, heart, and soul were simultaneously firing on all cylinders. I went from being *pushed* by unwelcome change to being *pulled forward* by possibility. By inspiration. By *aliveness*.

It wasn't all fun and games. I was also terrified. I was scared out of my mind to tell everyone I was leaving my "good" corporate job to try this unknown thing. I was afraid I would fail and have to come crawling back to the corporate world with my tail tucked between my legs. There were days when the fear would catch my heart and I could feel my throat closing inside me.

Aliveness was bigger than all of this. A gate had opened in my life. Beyond that doorway, I could see a shiny, more brilliant world—and I wanted to be in it. Forever.

That was over five years ago. I haven't completely followed aliveness for every decision in my business and life since then, but the outcomes have always been better when I did. When I choose to follow aliveness, I feel energized and have more traditional success. When I choose to follow what I'm supposed to do, I feel yucky, others don't connect with me, and I make less money. It's a bad combination.

You can use aliveness as a guide for your decisions as well. Notice if you feel alive while sitting in the lobby waiting for a job interview at a new company or in an exchange with your potential boss. Sense if you have the charge of aliveness when going on a date for the first time with someone you met online or while having coffee with a new friend. Pay attention to whether your current hobbies, activities, and relationships still feel alive for you—or if curiosity is pulling you elsewhere. Take a moment before saying yes or no to the project, party invitation, volunteer engagement, or job offer to see where aliveness is taking you, and THEN make your decision.

A Final Note about Aliveness

Throughout this chapter, we've gone into all the ways to follow aliveness. Before moving into the next chapter on trusting your knowing, I want to bring forward one more point about aliveness: Recognizing what deadens it.

Aliveness is a two-way street. It requires both following what makes you come alive and clearing out the grime that deadens your grounded wildness. I call The Break, "The Break" for a reason: You are breaking away from the rules that hold you down. You are letting go of the shame that was never yours to carry. You are releasing the old so there's space for the new to come rushing in. You are unlocking the weight on your wings so you can fly.

In the early spring of 2022, there was a small fire near a hiking trail I frequent in Boulder. Before I tell this story, let me point out that many fires in Colorado are destructive and devastating. They burn thousands of acres, leaving behind nothing but the charred trunks of pine trees that now look like toothpicks jutting out of the black earth. They take down homes and livelihoods. They aren't good.

This fire, however, was different from the catastrophes you often see on the news. Six weeks after the fire went through the open space, I was back on the trail. I stood above the area that had burned, surveyed what had happened, and noticed a strange thing: The ground the fire had burned was green.

Not just green, but *so much greener* than the areas that hadn't been touched by the fire. It was such a stark difference that a distinct line demarcated the exact stopping point of the fire. On the burned side, it was vibrant, green, and lush. On the unburned side, the overall hue was tan, with last year's brown grass interspersing with green shoots trying to break through.

The fire had cleared out all the dead stuff, leaving room for new growth. Leaving room for aliveness.

The same is true for you.

Go back to your Aliveness Agenda questions and flip them around. What are the people, places, and activities that dull your radiance? Are there people in your life who crush your soul and make you question yourself? Are there environments that bring on the weight of "should" and "supposed to"? Are there places in your life that suck the grounded wildness right out of you?

Notice. Then start clearing out. This isn't easy. We'll cover more on dealing with the repercussions of breaking away and clearing out in chapter 20.

And it's also okay. Whatever you might lose by letting go is simply a weight you never needed in the first place.

CHAPTER 16

Trust Your Knowing

(Even When It Doesn't Make Sense on Paper)

On October 1, 2020, I moved from Minnesota to Colorado.

I had grown up in Minnesota. I'd lived in other places in my early twenties and spent a year in Australia when I was thirty-three, but Minnesota was home. I had a large and amazing support network of friends there. I also had fantastic business contacts and a beautiful circle of women entrepreneurs. While I didn't have a huge family in Minnesota, my aunt and uncle were there all the time, along with my snowbird parents half the year.

I had a few friends in Colorado, but nothing like Minnesota. I also had zero business contacts and zero family there.

It was also during the heart of the coronavirus pandemic. And in the middle of the worst wildfire season on record in Colorado. Nothing about this move made sense on paper.

People would ask me why I was moving to Colorado. Was it for a job opportunity? A spouse's job opportunity? To be closer to family?

Nope. Nope. And nope.

I moved because I felt called to Colorado. I feel alive living next to the mountains and free beneath the wide-open skies. That was it.

Some people thought this was amazing. Others thought this decision was a little strange. Sometimes I thought it was a little strange, too!

Despite the complete and total lack of intellectual logic in my decision-making process, moving to Colorado was 100 percent the right thing to do. I felt at home the very first day I arrived.

Before you start to think this was an *easy* decision, however—that one day I just packed up my Honda Civic and drove through the plains until I reached the mountains—let me stop you. There was *a lot* of hesitation. *Years* of hesitation, in fact.

In 2005, I lived in Colorado for a year and only left because I had gotten into an excellent graduate program in Minnesota, where I could still get in-state tuition. I thought I would move back to Colorado the second I graduated with my master's degree. Instead, I got a great job in Minnesota and stayed.

When it was time to move on from that company, I applied for jobs in both Minnesota and Colorado. I got another great one in Minnesota and stayed. Then I started actively questioning moving again about a year after I left that corporate job. The questioning continued for another year, until I finally made the decision, packed up, and moved.

During that entire time, however, part of me longed to move to Colorado. Sometimes that longing was subtle, buried beneath busy jobs and social activities. Other times, the longing was fierce. I could sense my entire body reaching for the mountains. My journals are full of entries detailing this longing.

My knowing had had the answer for years. It saw that I needed to move to Colorado. I just didn't trust my knowing enough to take the risk and follow it sooner.

What Is Your Knowing?

Let's take a step back for a moment and give some definition to what I'm talking about when I say "your knowing."

There are many different words for your knowing. Some call it your intuition. Others refer to it as your spirit, soul, inner mentor, future self, guide, or sixth sense. They all mean the same thing.

In *An Overachiever's Guide to Breaking the Rules*, I referred to your inner knowing as your "true inner voice." I called it this in contrast to your inner critic, which often sounds like a critical, berating voice in your head. Unfortunately, calling it a voice confused a lot of people. Sometimes your inner knowing does speak to you in words you can hear even though no human is talking. This has happened to me once.

I was in my boss's office for a career development conversation, telling her I wanted to be a director, lead a team, and be involved in strategy. In the midst of my declarations, a voice came to me out of nowhere and said, *You are LYING right now.*

It was a poignant moment, to say the least! But this was ONE TIME. EVER. IN MY ENTIRE LIFE.

That day, my knowing decided to speak in actual words. Every other day of my life, however, my knowing has given me signals, clues, and answers without any words at all. Sometimes it shows up as a distressed feeling in my belly, guiding me away from a situation. If I'm journaling, it can arise in direct messages on the page I hadn't consciously known just a few moments earlier. Other times, I'm flooded with a vision of where I'm supposed to go in my life, and every fiber of my being knows it's the right path. And still other times, my knowing is just a question or curiosity. I don't know exactly what it means, but there's a pull I can't quite explain.

Your knowing may show up in similar ways, or it may come to you through different means. There's no right or wrong way to experience your knowing. The key is to pay attention to all the different ways it appears in your life—and then trust it enough to take steps along the path it's illuminating for you.

Trusting your knowing is as simple as YOU listening to YOU. So why is that so hard?

The Barriers to Your Knowing

We're all born with our knowing intact. For many of us,

however, our knowing gets lost during the years of performing. The rules you're handed tell you to ignore the signals of your body and trust *others'* voices more than any voice, feeling, or guidance inside of *you*. It can also be difficult to recognize what your knowing is telling you when you don't have the space to hear it in the first place.

You already know about creating space because you read an entire chapter on it! That space is intricately linked to trusting your knowing. You need it to hear yourself think, get a sense of what you desire, and feel what is right and wrong for you. If space is the main barrier to following your knowing, go back to chapter 13, read it again, and take another step to create space for yourself. It is the foundational practice for getting grounded and wild.

Logic also gets in the way of trusting your knowing. There's nothing wrong with logical thinking; however, most messages tell you it should be your *only* input for your decisions. The voice in your head has value, but so does the knowing of your heart and body. Instead of making decisions 95 percent from your head and 5 percent from your heart and body, you need to balance it out and give your knowing at least equal footing to your logical brain.

I've chosen logic over my knowing many times in my life—and they've never turned out well. When I first moved to Colorado, I stayed at an Airbnb for two months so that I'd have time to figure out where I wanted to live on a long-term basis. Shortly after arriving, I found a place to rent that seemed great on paper. It was semi furnished (a huge plus, since I had moved to Colorado with only the belongings that fit in my Honda Civic) and inexpensive (another plus, since my business had just started to legitimately do well and I didn't know whether it was a fluke or whether it would last). It was also in the basement of a house where a small family of three lived upstairs. They let me sign a six-month lease and were going to be away for the first two months, so I'd have the entire house to myself.

Immediately after signing the lease, my knowing showed up, telling me it was a bad idea. I got a nervous pit in my stomach whenever I thought about moving into the house. Everything in my body and heart told me to pump the brakes and get out of the lease, but I didn't have any logical reasons for these feelings, so I told myself it would be fine. I talked myself out of my knowing and kept the lease.

I regretted it within twenty-four hours of moving in. I knew basement living wasn't ideal, but I hadn't understood the immediate impact of living in a cavern. I felt trapped. I longed to gaze out at the blue sky and see a ray of sunshine cascade on the floor. The only way I could get that, however, was to stand directly next to a window, crane my neck, and look straight up.

Then the basement flooded. My entire kitchen floor was covered in a watery mixture of who knows what (and I really don't want to know what). The landlord, who was now away for those two months, called a plumber and got it fixed quickly. But it wasn't fun.

Then the mice arrived. I heard them scurrying around in the ceiling panels above me, a whole family of critters making their home in my home. The landlord again took action quickly and called an exterminator, who opted to put out poison instead of setting traps. A few days after the poison was distributed, I saw a mouse clambering around my kitchen floor, looking sick and drunk. The poison had started the job but hadn't finished it. That became my duty.

Here's the real kicker: The landlord had forgotten to tell me they were going to sublet out the upstairs while they were gone. Three weeks after I moved in, at 2:00 a.m. on Christmas, a family of five arrived and took up residence above me. They were the nicest people you'll ever meet, but I learned quickly that every single sound they made traveled directly to me. I heard every word of every conversation in their kitchen, even with my door closed. Every footstep reverberated through the floors and woke me up, so I could only sleep when all of them were sleeping, which was definitely not my required eight hours a night.

On December 30, five days after the family of five moved in, I called my landlord and told him I couldn't stay. I was exhausted and unhappy. I had to get out, no matter what. We decided it was fair for me to pay a total of three months of the lease. I immediately started looking for a new place. I moved out three weeks later and paid double rent for the agreed-upon remaining time.

All because I valued logic over my knowing.

Of course, my knowing didn't tell me there was going to be a flood, mice, or unending noise. But it knew something was wrong. It gave me all the signals, and I chose not to listen. I've now learned that's never a good idea.

Then there's the next scenario: You're in touch with

your knowing. You've loosened up the requirement for logic. You're feeling connected to yourself. Good on you!

Then your knowing asks you to take a risk. It gives you a signal, loud and clear, to do something unexpected. It tells you to quit your stable job and start a business, sell the condo you've owned for ten years and start renting again, move across the country, and write a book that may blow up everything in your business.*

When that happens, the rules you've been taught often snap back into place, heeding you to take the path well-traveled. They tell you that it's risky and scary, and that there's no good reason to make a change. They remind you how you're "supposed to" show up to be a good woman, mother, partner, daughter, friend, employee, and leader; and they flood you with waves of guilt for breaking away from that definition.

Chances are good that actual, real people are also questioning your knowing and the direction you're taking in life. Most often it's with good intention, but underlying that positive intent may be a deep discomfort within themselves about the decision you're making. After all, they've been handed rules as well—and just watching another person break them can be unsettling.

Breaking the norms you've been taught is uncomfortable, plain and simple. Especially if you've spent most of your life conforming through proving, pleasing, and perfecting.

---

*   That's my life and this book I'm talking about!

The discomfort goes a layer deeper than breaking the rules, though. Sometimes it's just straight-up scary to follow your knowing. Thinking about leaving my job to start a business induced borderline panic attacks. I thought I might throw up the day I walked into my manager's office to give my notice. And that was before I had even started the business. *Running* a business has asked me to leap outside my comfort time and time again.

For example, writing my first book felt amazing in so many ways—and some pieces were vulnerable and scary to share. This book takes that vulnerability up a million notches. When I moved to Colorado, I wondered if I would be lonely, lose business, and find a place to live that I liked. Turned out I was lonely occasionally, although not any more often than I felt lonely in Minnesota. My business only continued to grow after moving. And while finding a good place to live didn't work out so well the first time around, I'm happy to share that the second try has been a winner!

Yes, it can be uncomfortable to follow your knowing. It's also beautiful. And wonderful. Your knowing will take you places you never thought possible. You will experience a freedom that performing could never give you. You will feel the power of creating your own rules for life.

You will be grounded and wild.

How to Start Following Your Knowing

Hearing, trusting, and acting on your knowing is a practice—and one that gets easier over time. For years, I felt partially disconnected from my deep inner knowing. When I first started actively listening to my knowing, it mostly gave me hunches and nudges without any directions. Instead of a clear message, it was more of a feeling that made me pause and think, *I should pay attention to this. I don't know what it means, but it means something.*

Then I started to get questions—without immediate answers. For example, I knew with total certainty that my job had to change at the end of my corporate career. I didn't know right away, though, that I would start a business. I considered many different options before my knowing gave me a clear path forward into entrepreneurship.

Over time, the distance between questions and answers has shortened. So much so that sometimes they come at the same time! Other times, however, big questions and rumblings need to percolate before answers and next steps arise.

Through all of this, I've found three approaches particularly helpful to following my knowing. None of these practices are check-the-box items you can put on a to-do list and complete. Your knowing doesn't work that way anyway! Instead, they are mindset shifts, reminders, and means that offer a path back to your knowing.

Give Yourself Permission

During my speaking engagements, I often talk about giving yourself permission. For example, give yourself permission to set a boundary. Give yourself permission to say no. Give yourself permission to lower the bar. Give yourself permission to let go of the rules you've been handed and create your own rules for life. You may remember that giving yourself permission is the first step to feeling your feelings as well.

Permission is like the key to a locked door. Without the key, you can push and shove into that door as much as you want and it won't open. Giving yourself permission is stopping the fight against the door, taking a breath, and slipping in the key. You still have to decide to open the door and walk through, but the fight is over.

In this metaphor, the fight is with the door. In life, the fight for permission is with yourself. That fight doesn't originate from inside you (the rules you were taught are responsible for that), but it does have to end inside you. If you're waiting for someone else to come along and tell you it's okay to trust yourself and follow your knowing, you will likely be waiting a long time. You might get lucky and have a friend, mentor, or partner who encourages you. But even then, you need to make the decision. Only you have the power to give yourself permission.

Start there. Start with giving yourself permission to listen to yourself.

Get Curious and Play

Consider this scenario: Your knowing gives you a clear message that something in your job needs to change. Immediately, your inner critic jumps in to counter your knowing. Maybe it sounds something like this:

Change my job? But this was the job I thought I wanted! At the company I always wanted to work for! That doesn't make any sense! It would be ridiculous to leave this job. And what would I do anyway? Is there even anything else better out there for me? What would other people think if I left this job? They'd think I was being ridiculous, too! And what if I do something different, and I totally regret it? Or worse, what if I flop on my face and fail? No. I should just be grateful for this job and stop paying attention to the dumb voice telling me to make a change.

Any of that sound familiar? You can see all the barriers we talked about earlier in this chapter shoving themselves into your inner monologue. The rules, valuing logic above all else, worrying about what other people will think more than listening to your knowing, the discomfort of trying something new—they're all in there.

This happens all the time. You judge your knowing to be wrong before you've had a chance to explore it. You shut down questions before the answers have time to arise. You cut off the whisper behind your heart before it can gain volume and confidence.

Instead of judging your knowing, ask questions. Compassionate, curious, open-ended questions, like the ones required to go from breaking down to breaking open. That same approach goes for following your knowing outside of a big break. Those questions can sound like this:

- What do I know about this feeling?
- What am I curious about exploring?
- Where am I being pulled?
- What am I longing for?
- What questions do I have about the message my knowing is sending?
- What's the next right thing to do?

Then start to play.

Yes, you heard that right. PLAY.

It's easy to feel like you have to make the right decision when you believe every forward action is permanent. With that approach, then you better have every single piece of information available before you take the first step. You better cross all your t's and dot all your i's to eliminate all possible margins for error, mistakes, and failure.

I get stressed out just thinking about it. The weight of all that pressure is too much to bear. It can feel easier to ignore your knowing and keep marching forward in the status quo than to explore where your knowing is pulling you.

Play, on the other hand, feels light. You get to try something and see how you like it, without any strings attached. You get to have a conversation, take a class, or ask to be on the team heading up a new project, and then you see what happens.

You don't have to know if you want the job when you apply for it. You have the entire interview process to figure that out! You also don't have to know if you want to publish a book when you get a pull to explore writing. All you have to do is sign up for the low-key, inexpensive community ed writing class and see what you think. You don't have to know if you want to leave the city and live in the country when you start craving more quiet. Start by spending a week at an Airbnb in the country and notice how you feel during your stay.

You don't have to know the end at the beginning. All you have to do is get curious and play.

Let Things Emerge

In July 2020, I took a trip to Colorado to decide if I wanted to move there. I assumed I would have a clear answer after my five days of backpacking in the mountains and another five days to explore towns north of Denver where I could potentially live. After all, I'd been thinking about this decision actively for months—and inactively for years! I thought all I needed was to set foot in Colorado and look around, and then my knowing would show up and guide the way.

It didn't.

I drove away from Colorado back to Minnesota, still about 90 percent sure I wanted to make the move, but not the 100 percent I had expected. Even thirteen hours of solo driving across cornfields with nothing to do but contemplate my decision didn't make my knowing show up and give me an answer.

I was frustrated. What else did I need to make this decision? What was holding me back? I didn't like this in-between feeling. I wanted an answer—now!

I stewed in that discouraged sense of ambiguity for a few days. And then my knowing showed up!

I was sitting outside on my patio journaling as sunset turned to dusk and then to darkness. The outdoor light behind me illuminated the journal pages just enough that I could keep writing.

In that writing, I realized I had come back to a home in Minnesota I didn't belong to anymore. I was already in transition without even knowing it. The next chapter of my life was calling me. All I had to do was turn the page.

As I continued to write, the decision emerged with total clarity. I wrote:

> The decision is made. I am moving. There is no if. I am moving to Colorado. Maybe I just need to keep writing it again and again. **I am moving to Colorado.** I'm turning the page to the next chapter. And now, as I write these words, I am smiling. The fear is morphing into excitement right now as I write. An involuntary smile is on my lips. Because I know this is right. I'm giddy and free, and tears are almost coming to my eyes. This is right. I am moving to Colorado.

Sometimes things need a little time to mix and meld—and *then* they will emerge. Yes, this space in between can be uncomfortable. It's annoying when you have a rumbling in your belly telling you something is coming, but you don't know what that something is, how it's going to show up, or when it's going to appear. It's frustrating when you want an answer NOW, but the answer isn't ready to present itself. You may even feel a bit untethered, like you're leaping between what was and what will be without solid ground beneath you.

When this happens, allow yourself to be uncomfortable. Feel your feelings. Sit in the discomfort so that you can move in the direction of your knowing instead of running back to the safety of what is familiar.

Remind yourself that you are your own grounding. You belong within. You are enough, worthy, and whole.

You don't have to prove that you can follow your knowing and make this leap in record time, landing perfectly on both feet on the very first try.

You can give yourself permission to trust the journey of your knowing. You can throw off the notion that everything has to be completely logical and make sense according to the rules our culture has deemed acceptable. You can get curious, play, and see what happens. The path will emerge in front of you as you walk forward.

It will be YOUR path. Wild and grounded in YOU. Not the life that's been handed to you by your family, not the life your boss wants for you, not the life you're "supposed to" have. It will be YOUR life. YOUR path. YOUR truth.

And that is worth everything.

CHAPTER 17

Let Your Body Lead

In 2019, I slowly gained ten pounds. My jeans were a little tight, but that was about it. I doubt it was even noticeable to anyone but me.

An interesting thing happened with this weight gain, though. It was something that had never happened before: When I glanced in the mirror, I thought I looked fine.

I wasn't sassing and flirting with myself like I did after my second break. But when I surveyed my body, I felt neutral about it. Occasionally even positive.

This was a marked difference from my previous weight

gains, when shame and self-loathing would have set in immediately. Instead of looking at my body with neutrality, I would have analyzed every roll on my stomach, questioning with criticism just how much bigger I had gotten. I would have noticed with horror as my belly protruded over my jeans and grazed against the inside of my shirt, making it obvious I had a ring of fat around my middle.

At first, I thought this new reaction was because I truly did look "better" than I had with previous weight gains. I had been doing strength exercises consistently for several months. Perhaps some of the weight I had gained was muscle. Or perhaps the new strength was holding the extra weight in, allowing for a better self-perception according to what I'd been taught a "good" body is supposed to look like.

Then I realized that none of this was true. It wasn't that my body looked different than it had in the past at this same weight. Instead, the change was internal. I simply didn't hate my body anymore. This was a massive shift from the previous thirty years of my life.

I went on my first diet at age eleven, when I was at a perfectly healthy weight. I checked off boxes of protein, dairy, fruits, and carbohydrates in accordance with whatever WeightWatchers plan was used in 1991. I didn't go to an actual WeightWatchers meeting, and this first attempt at dieting didn't last long, but already I felt like there was something wrong with my body, and I had to fix it.

That desire to fix my body tumbled into outright shame when I gained thirty pounds in my first semester of seventh grade. I hated my body. HATED it. I was ashamed of the rolls around my stomach and the staring eyes of boys as my DDD breasts bounced down the hallway of my middle school. I was embarrassed by the fact that I wore a size 14 jeans when it seemed like everyone around me was wearing a size 6—or smaller.

Even more so, I was ashamed of *myself* for not losing weight. I felt like there was something wrong with me for eating too much and not being able to control what I put in my mouth. My outward body was a visual representation of the shame I felt on the inside, which made me hate it even more. This was the one area of my life where I was completely and totally failing, and I couldn't stand it.

For decades, I worked to control my weight through external means. I counted calories burned on the Stair-Master and calories consumed through various weight loss programs. I felt like I had to rely on external tools because I couldn't possibly know how to feed and care for myself based on following my own needs and intuition. I believed my body couldn't be trusted to send me the right signals about food and eating—and that I couldn't be trusted to follow those messages even if they were accurate.

To be fair, I wasn't well. I don't know if I had a diagnosable eating disorder, but I absolutely had disordered eating. I regularly binged to the point of physical pain. Had I thrown up that binge, everyone would have called it bulimia. But I didn't, so whatever I was doing went unnamed.

Something in me needed to be *healed*, but nothing in me needed to be *fixed*. The problem wasn't a lack of willpower or self-control. The problem was the rules I'd been handed that had taught me to be ashamed in the first place. The problem was all the proving, pleasing, and perfecting that required the release valve I got through binging. The problem was the message that I had to fix my body to be a whole, worthy, desirable woman. The problem was the overarching directive that my body couldn't be trusted. Instead, it was something to contain and control.

It took me a long time to recognize the real problems. Losing weight didn't make it happen. Even becoming aware of all the rules hasn't made it sink in entirely. I will admit that the messages telling me what my body is supposed to look like have been the hardest ones to truly break free from.

I'm no longer ashamed of my body. I believe my body is desirable. I don't feel like I have to prove myself to men in other ways to make up for a less-than-perfect body. I know I'm healthy, and that's really all that should matter. But . . .

I still frequently feel like I should lose ten pounds. Some days I look at myself naked in the mirror, and I want my stomach to be flatter. I'm happy when the number on the scale goes down and when my jeans feel loose. I get frustrated that my feminist, supposedly enlightened, grounded, and wild self can't seem to 100 percent kick this set of bullshit rules to the curb and be done with them forever. And yet, they persist.

That's how deep this is buried.

I know I'm not alone here. Last year, I was hiking with a friend, and I mentioned this journey, saying, "I'm not ashamed of my body anymore, but I still think about it all the time.

I think about what I'm eating and how often and if I should lose weight and all those things."

My friend's response? "So you're like a normal American woman now."

She was right, assuming we define "normal" as what most women are thinking, feeling, and experiencing. Nearly all of us have been enculturated with the notion that our bodies are wrong somehow and in need of constant fixing, regardless of our personal journey with weight. There's always some part that could be tighter or softer, longer or leaner, curvier or stronger, with whiter teeth, fewer wrinkles, and smoother skin.

All this shame, fixing, and controlling leads to a deeper issue: disconnection from our bodies. Through years of following the rules, your body becomes an enemy that gets in the way of your plans and productivity. You learn to ignore pain, disregard exhaustion, and push through sickness. You drink coffee instead of sleeping. You eat meal replacement bars to lose weight. You force yourself to get through your to-do list when everything in you *longs* to lie on the couch and rest.

That's just the negative side of the spectrum. Most of us are also taught to disconnect from pleasure, from small acts like slowing down to enjoy the juicy ecstasy of a freshly picked plum still warm from the sun's heat or noticing the pleasant way your hips move as you walk down the street, to bigger dives into pleasure like allowing yourself to fully succumb to the wild nature of your body during sex.

I was disconnected from my body's most basic signals

for years. I had a "work hard, play hard" attitude, which basically meant I was sleep-deprived a good portion of the time from age fifteen until my late thirties, when I finally made sleep a priority in my life. I forced myself to exercise five to six days a week, no matter how my body felt. I fought against hunger and got mad at my body when I didn't think it "should" be hungry.

Disconnection from these basic signals blocked me from working with my body on a deeper level as well. I ignored the pits of anxiety that frequently arose in my belly. I chalked up the constant tightness in my shoulders, back, and hips to stress without investigating the underlying causes. I didn't know enough to think about tapping into my body to make decisions, let alone follow the insights my body gave me.

Looking back, this all makes sense. Why would I listen to this thing I hated so much? Why would I want a deeper connection to a body that had caused me so much shame?

Little did I know that the combination of recognizing the rules handed to me and reconnecting to my body would be a cure for that shame. Breaking down the rules we've discussed was step one. That first shift led to rediscovering joy in my body and then to letting my body lead, a journey that continues today.

Unleash Joy in Your Body

When I started working on this section, I titled it, "Find Joy in Your Body," but that didn't feel quite right. I wanted to convey release and freedom, and *find* just wasn't doing it.

So, like any writer, I jumped to an online thesaurus, typed *release*, and scanned the synonyms. As soon as I saw the word *unleash*, I knew that was it.

It's time to stop trying to control your body.

It's time to let go of contempt and hatred toward your body.

It's time to release the shame you've been taught about your body not being "right."

It's time to let go of embarrassment for desiring pleasure.

It's time to *unleash joy*. Pure, unbridled, uncontrolled joy. Grounded joy. *Wild* joy.

It's time to be free in your body, which will automatically make you free in yourself.

How? The answer is your response to one simple question: What makes you feel both grounded *and* wild in your body?

For me, the first answer is dance. Dance has been the gateway to not just *tolerate* my body, but also *enjoy* it.

Let me be clear here: I have zero skills as a dancer. I didn't take dance classes as a kid. I was never in the center of a circle, showing off my moves at a high school dance. If someone pushed me into the spotlight, I *ran* back and disappeared into the safety of the crowd as fast as my scurrying legs could take me.

Dancing is not about skill for me. It's not about having the steps right or looking good. It's not about being in total rhythm with the music. And it's definitely not about having a partner.

Dancing is about letting go in the most physical way. Some days, I turn on a fast song and whip my hands around like they're soaking wet and I'm trying to get every last drop of water off them. I drive my knees to my chest and shake my head back and forth like I'm in some sort of deranged '80s exercise video. I gallop around my living room and laugh at myself.

I assure you, it's not a pretty, neat, put-together sight. But it is *joyful*.

On other days, I put on a slower song with deep tones and feel my body decelerate to the tempo of the melody. I enjoy the sensuality of my hips swirling back and forth without having to prove that sensuality to anyone. I sense the power emanating from my lower belly and pelvis as they move with the music.

I become *grounded* in myself as I dance. I sink into my body and the earth beneath my feet.

I'm also *wild*. I dance with freedom, fire, boldness, and JOY.

There is no shame. There are no rules. They melt into the background, and I come back into my body—and back into myself.

Dance was the first way I learned to unleash joy in my body. I've since learned to notice it in everyday situations, like when the wind comes up on a walk and I reach my arms wide and open myself to the freedom that exists in the air. Or when I'm playing my guitar and belting out the words to a Joni Mitchell or Brandi Carlile song. I sing from the top of my head, the center of my heart, and the deepest part of my belly all at the same time. I feel the power of my voice as I release deeper into my body.

I unleash joy in my body, which in turn reconnects me to myself.

What does this for you? What makes *you* feel grounded and wild in your body?

If you aren't sure, experiment. Your Aliveness Agenda may give you clues. Wherever you start, I recommend doing something no one else can see. You don't want any element of performing in your practice to unleash joy. You can't feel free in your body while thinking about needing to prove, please, perfect, or even rebel. It's just not going to happen. So shut your door and close your blinds—or get into a secluded spot in nature—and let your body be FREE.

If it still feels awkward to let yourself go, that's okay. It's a process to release your body when you've been working to control it for most of your life. You will get there. And it will feel amazing.

Let Your Body Lead

Letting your body lead is the next level—and one that I'm working on every day. It means listening to your body, trusting its signals, and acting based on those signals. Even when logic is telling you to do something different. Even when it's scary to follow the knowing of your body. Even when the rules are pushing you to make a different decision.

Here's a small example: This week, I had time set aside on a Tuesday morning to write. When I woke up that day, my body had other ideas. My jaw and belly were tight. My mind was tired and foggy. Part of me (the old rule follower part) wanted to push through and force myself to sit down and write. To be honest, I was annoyed! I was frustrated that my body wasn't lining up with my schedule. I also knew from experience that forcing doesn't work. I knew that I needed to let my body lead and that I'd eventually come back to writing.

I first took a short walk to get some fresh air. Then I danced to a fast song or two. After that, my body told me I didn't need to go fast; instead, I needed to slow down. I switched to downtempo songs and continued to move around my living room as my intuition guided me. Then I felt a need to simply lie down. I grabbed a blanket and plopped myself on the floor. I stretched occasionally if my body asked for it, but mostly I just laid there.

Half an hour later, I was back. The tightness in my jaw and belly had disappeared. My mind had cleared, and my energy had returned. I'd missed my entire writing block—but on the flip side, I'd gotten an idea for this chapter while lying on the floor that reshaped its entire messaging.

I let my body lead, and it led me in the right direction. It always does.

This goes way beyond knowing when to slow down and take breaks. My body told me it was a bad idea to sign the lease on the basement apartment. It floods with a calm joy when I have a great new idea for my business. It lets me know when I'm holding back my voice and urges me to step into my fullness. It sends me guidance about whether I should go on a date with a guy and whether that first date should be followed by a second.

Your body will do the same for you. It will guide

you to speak your truth. It will show you the right (and wrong!) decision to make. It will tell you when you need to stop and take a breath. It will direct you to the next step in your career. It will show you how to claim yourself and take up space, which are covered in the next chapters.

In short, your body will lead you back to yourself. Every time I let my body lead is a step away from performing and a step back into my natural instincts. A step further into freedom. A step deeper into grounded wildness.

CHAPTER 18

Claim Yourself

When I was thirty-one, I wrote a poem titled "Red Heels and Black Lace." Here is one of the stanzas:

> Always happy, laughing, smiling,
> That's what you expect of me.
> Rosy cheeks, freckles, clear blue eyes,
> One-sided picture that you see.

I have always been a nice girl—and that is a real part of me! I'm happy, laughing, and smiling pretty darn frequently. I love to play games and sing songs. I'm regularly filled to the brim with joy and wonder. I LOVE my freckles! They're more than colorations on my skin; they're a part of who I am.

I call this part of me Sweet Girl.

But there's another part of me too. I call her Fire.

Fire rocks the boat with zero fear. Fire takes risks and bucks the status quo. Fire climbs out to the farthest rock just to know how it feels to be on the edge. Fire stands in her value and says no when someone tries to convince her to do a speaking engagement for free. Fire was the one who stopped her date under an umbrella in the middle of a downpour to make out.

Throughout my life, both Sweet Girl and Fire have been encouraged by the people around me. My parents and most of my teachers invited me to speak my mind. The leaders at my church when I was growing up supported me when I asked questions. Friends told me they liked it when my spontaneous and adventurous side came out. I've received as much praise for my boldness and willingness to take risks as I have for being "nice."

Fire, however, has also received criticism. She has been told she's too direct. She was given instructions to sit on her hands in meetings to remind her to slow down. She was told to shush by the guy she was dating when her voice got too loud. Fire has been questioned when she's made decisions to work less, disregard traditional sales approaches, and generally do things differently from the way you're "supposed to" do them to run a successful business. And she has gotten surprised, confused, and sometimes judging looks when she has pushed back.

Because of this, I learned to be cautious of Fire. I came to understand that Sweet Girl was *always* welcome, and that

Fire was not. I became afraid that Fire would be rejected and criticized if let her fully loose, so I contained her. I knew this when I wrote another stanza for the poem:

> A fire coiling and reeling,
> Pulsing just below the skin.
> Heat rises up, I push it down,
> Never quite allow it in.

Claiming myself has been a process to allow Fire to rise to the top and live alongside Sweet Girl. It's been the journey of inviting the eight-year-old holding the snake to live in my forty-something-year-old body. Her bold, calm confidence is the ultimate blend of Sweet Girl and Fire. They are both a part of me, swirling around inside my soul, making decisions about how to show up in the world.

What's more, they balance each other out. Sweet Girl is the yin to Fire's yang. Fire pushes the boundaries and speaks her mind, and Sweet Girl makes sure Fire does so in an inclusive way where others have a chance to be heard as well. Fire goes her own way, and Sweet Girl reminds her that everyone's way is different. Fire embraces her anger and determination. Sweet Girl remembers to stay curious, ask questions, and listen.

Being all Fire would be as unhealthy and ungrounded as being all Sweet Girl. All Fire is rebelling. All Sweet Girl is proving, pleasing, and perfecting. I need them both to *live* my life instead of *perform* it.

Learning to integrate Sweet Girl and Fire has been a quest of claiming my fire—and then living both sides of me out loud in the world. Sweet Girl didn't need to be claimed; she was already fully mature and free. It was Fire who needed to be stoked. It was Fire who needed oxygen to breathe. It was Fire who needed to be let loose.

Claiming myself as both Sweet Girl and Fire is my living definition of grounded wildness. When I integrate both sides of me, I am free to fly because I am grounded in my spirit. I am both untamed and centered by an unshakeable core. I am all of me, out in the world, all of the time.

Because of Fire's past experiences, it's still an active decision every day to uncage her and let her loose. I know I can let Fire out even more without her overtaking Sweet Girl—and I'm working on it. Some days, I keep Fire reined in because it's vulnerable to fully liberate her. She is still more likely to get criticized. I still worry sometimes that Fire will be rejected by clients, friends, and men. The world is not yet used to *any* woman showing up in her Fire, which means it isn't used to *me* showing up in my Fire, either.

What's also true is that I'm tired. I'm tired of holding myself back. I'm tired of constraining my Fire. I'm tired of censoring my voice to make it more palatable. I'm tired of asking questions instead of challenging directly. I'm tired of wondering if my messages will be accepted by corporate culture. I'm tired of toning down my emotions. I'm tired of denying myself to make others more comfortable.

And so, I claim my Fire. I claim her as I claim my freedom. As I claim my grounded wildness.

You have to claim yourself as well. All the other practices we've discussed funnel into this moment. Creating space allows you to pause and listen to your authentic self. Feeling your feelings without judgment and following aliveness bring you back into your fullness. Trusting your knowing and letting your body lead are the internal practices of claiming yourself.

Now it's time to bring it all together and declare exactly who you are. This is you separate from the rules you've been handed. Separate from "should" and "supposed to." Separate from the definitions you've been told about what it means to be a good girl, woman, and person. This is your version of Fire and Sweet Girl alive in the world, no matter how much your fire has been doused over the years.

You're going to proclaim yourself, in actual words. I did this exercise last year, at a time when I needed an anchor that connected who I was on the inside and how I was showing up in the world on the outside. I wanted words that embodied both Fire and Sweet Girl so I could remind myself of who I am—and so I could consciously unleash Fire, even when it's uncomfortable.

I started by reflecting on what I was being called to share and the intentions for my work. I thought about what I desired and my definition of success. I leaned into everything I am, both my Fire and my Sweet Girl.

Then I put a stake in the ground. I claimed myself with these words:

- I am a woman who challenges the status quo.
- I am a woman who never just takes what she can get.
- I am a woman who lives in her fullness without apology.
- I am a woman who breaks the rules *with* purpose.
- I am a woman who uses my voice for change.

- I am a woman who listens and sees people for all of who they are without my own agenda.
- I am a woman who lives in joy and wonder.
- I am a woman who is free and ALIVE.

This is me. All of me. Sweet Girl *and* Fire.

This is also me internally *and* externally. Most of what we've covered so far in this book has been internal. We've discussed breaking the rules that lead to shame and reclaiming your worth so that you can step into grounded wildness. This is deep change—and change always starts on the inside.

At some point, though, you need to live into your fullness OUT LOUD. You can't do the work of knowing who you are and then hide it for the rest of your life. You need to take a stand, stop performing, and LIVE.

That's where your "I Am a Woman Who . . ." declarations come into play. They are the definition of who you are internally—and how that person will show up in the world.

While there is no right or wrong way to declare yourself, I highly recommend using the phrase "I am a woman who . . ." or "I am a person who . . ." or any other noun that fits your identity. Simply using "I am . . ." will often lead to the titles of your life, like mother, partner, friend, volunteer, daughter, aunt, leader, or your actual job title. You are more than these simplistic titles, and I want you to see yourself beyond them. I challenge you to identify a deeper version of who you are and describe how your unleashed self will be visible in the world.

That may be enough instruction for you. Perhaps your

proclamations have already shown up as you've been read-ing, and they're now written in the margins of these pages! If you'd like more structure, however, here's what I recommend:

1. Create space for yourself by blocking thirty minutes (or longer!) just for you. If you live with other people (e.g., a partner, kids, parents, roommates), arrange a time to have them out of the house or leave the house yourself. Silence your phone. Give yourself the gift of uninterrupted space.

2. Do a short activity that clears your head and helps you feel like yourself. This may be a walk outside, dancing to a fun song, savoring a cup of tea, or simply closing your eyes and breathing for a few minutes.

3. Open your journal or grab a blank sheet of paper. At the top, write the words, "I am a woman/person/ etc. who . . ."

4. Set a timer for ten minutes.

5. Write continuously for those ten minutes, allowing whatever comes up to land on the page. Don't pick up your pen. Don't worry about spelling, grammar, or even if everything you're writing makes sense. Don't censor a single word. Let it all out. This method of continuous writing is powerful because it unearths thoughts buried in your subconscious mind.

6. When the timer goes off, keep writing if you're in the middle of something good, or finish your last sentence and take a breath. Read through what you wrote, underlining anything that stands out to you as the person you are, fully claimed.

7. Write your final "I am a woman/person/etc. who . . ." declarations. You may have three, or you may have ten. There is no set number of statements to describe who you are. Also, release any notion that these have to be the permanent statements that describe you for the rest of your life. If a new statement arises tomorrow, add it in!* If one of the statements doesn't feel right later, take it out. You are rediscovering yourself by doing this exercise (and everything else in this book), and this is a process that never ends. You always get to evolve and change.

8. Read the declarations to yourself in the mirror— OUT LOUD. Lean into the words. Say them with strength, even if it feels awkward. You can smile, laugh, and flirt with yourself as well; it doesn't all have to be heavy and serious! No matter your tenor, look yourself in the eyes, say the words, and *claim yourself.*

And then, live into your declarations. Live as the full, embodied, true, wholehearted woman you are. Live into your newly claimed self, let the world see your fire, and *take up space*.

Which is exactly what's coming next.

---

* I recently added "I am a woman who has hard conversations" to my list and that declaration has given me the courage and motivation I needed to have those conversations.

CHAPTER 19

Take up Space

As I began to claim myself and step into grounded wildness, a familiar feeling crept into my body: the discomfort of moving into a bigger space.

The feeling itself was nothing new. I felt it in a big way when I contemplated leaving my corporate job to start a business. There were moments when excitement and possibility took the lead, and I had glimpses of what my life and work could be like. I saw myself publishing books, standing on a stage, and talking about important things I hoped would make a difference. These visions were as clear as day.

Inevitably, though, after these moments of clarity, the inner critic would show up with the dreaded "Just who do you think you are?" commentary. "Just who do you think you are to go off and start a business?" it would say to me. "Aren't you a little big for your britches, thinking you can write a book and get paid to speak on stages and believe what you say will make a difference?"

These doubting thoughts often get labeled as imposter syndrome, and that is an accurate description for some people. That wasn't happening to me, though. (At least not in these moments! I've experienced imposter syndrome at other times.) I wasn't doubting my qualifications, knowledge, or capability to do the work. (That would be imposter syndrome.) Instead, the inner critic was trying to keep me safe from stepping into this new, uncomfortable, and sometimes downright terrifying experience of leaving my job and starting a business. It was trying to guard me from the discomfort of taking up space and living my truth out loud.

As I got into running my business, this discomfort shifted away from the simple fear of launching to the uneasiness of putting myself out there as a teacher and expert. When I stepped onto stages, I felt both the healthy responsibility of having an audience and the idea of, "Holy crap, that's a whole lot of people who are going to listen to me. Isn't it a little *arrogant* of me to think I should be up on this stage?"

Arrogance may have been the fear the inner critic presented to me, but I've learned that the core is more nuanced. In reality, I'm afraid that sharing my truth and experiences will come across as me knowing it all and having everything figured out. I'm afraid I will use the power I have on stage (or on my podcast or in social media posts) as a power *over* others. I fear I will come across as the unhealthy definition

of power we've seen in so many of our leaders throughout history.

When that happens, I remind myself that these are good
questions to ask. However, just the fact that I'm asking them
likely means I'm not lording my power over anyone. People
who truly are arrogant and use their power in toxic ways typically aren't pausing to reflect on it. They just march forward,
living up to past definitions of what power was supposed
to look like.

By taking up space in a different way, I get to be a part
of changing that definition of power. I get to lead in a wholehearted, inclusive way. I get to be in power *with* people,
as opposed to using power *over* them.

It's a complete flip of my fears. Instead of feeling the discomfort of taking up space, it becomes an honor to play a role
in creating change.

As I continued to let go of performing and break through
into grounded wildness, the discomfort of being called into
a bigger space spread out to other parts of my life as well.
During my second big break, I uncaged Fire to live alongside Sweet Girl. I broke away from the shame caused
by all the rules telling me I wasn't desirable and started
to believe in my radiance. It was an internal game, but inevitably others noticed. People started mentioning how free
and happy I looked. They commented that I was clearly
in my element and loving life when I shared posts on social
media. Most of them chalked it up to moving to Colorado,
but I knew a deeper change was in play.

Then there were men. In a matter of months, I went

from feeling invisible to being noticed *all of the time*. I'd be at the counter of a brewery, ordering a beer, and suddenly the guy sitting a few seats down would strike up a conversation. I bought new windshield wipers from an auto parts store, and the clerk offered to put them on my car—but there was no sign in the store stating that they did these kinds of tasks. He just did it. Free of charge. Without me even asking for it.

One day, I walked into the post office, carrying both a large box of copies of *An Overachiever's Guide to Breaking the Rules* and a basket overflowing with several small packages of books to ship out. A man not only opened the door for me, but he also stopped to compliment me on the beautiful way I walked. Let's be clear—there was no way I was even remotely graceful walking into that post office, trying to balance all my boxes. And yet, there was something he sensed in me.

You know the poem "Phenomenal Woman" by Maya Angelou? If not, go read it now. It's magnificent. I have always loved that poem, but it felt like a fantasy for me. Perhaps other women could embody the mysterious confidence she captured in the poem. But me? Nope.

And yet, there I was, becoming a phenomenal woman.

And it. Was. WEIRD.

I both loved it and wanted to push it away.

I felt like I had been living inside a cocoon for years and was finally transforming into a butterfly. I looked the same on the outside, but inside it was a complete metamorphosis. It was uncomfortable to break loose and let myself out into the world after living within both the comfort and the constriction of the cocoon. I had to get used to living with this freedom, even though I had longed for it ever since losing my wildness in seventh grade. I had to practice taking up space and living as the phenomenal woman I was.

The Rules That Make It Uncomfortable

Before we get into practicing, let's talk about the rules that make it so uncomfortable for us to take up space. Because doesn't it always come back to those rules—and dismantling them to live your truth?

The messages women have gotten about taking up space are confusing and conflicting. They tell you to break the glass ceiling—but to do so softly, without offending anyone. They encourage you to follow your dreams and live your best life—as long as it doesn't upset or disappoint people. They advise you to be bold and confident and speak up—and then they give you "constructive" feedback for being direct, bossy, or angry when you follow that advice. At times, it can feel easier to stay quiet and shrink.

There's another worry I see pop up for many women. It's well-intentioned, but it still has the result of diminishing you. It's the fear that putting yourself out there, in all your glory, will make other people feel small. A worry that stepping into your allotted space will take space away from others.

This is a challenging one because we've all seen examples where space *is* taken away. It happens every time someone is interrupted, which happens to women *much* more frequently than men. It occurs when a colleague takes credit for the work their team member completed. It takes place when a boss presents the work of their employee and gets all the recognition for their fantastic ideas.

We need to be aware that this happens and purposefully engage in practices that allow everyone to have a voice. We need to address the microaggressions that shut down underrepresented voices, like interruptions, undue questioning, and tone policing. We need to give credit where credit is due.

At the same time, know that sharing your strengths does not squash anyone else's strengths. Speaking your truth does not silence anyone else's truth. Letting your fire out into the world does not douse the flames of the people around you. You are allowed to show your radiance and step into the space you have been allocated as a human being.

Finally, it's vulnerable to take up space. Even if you weren't handed all these rules and conflicting messages, it would still be vulnerable to put yourself out there. Sharing yourself means opening yourself up to criticism, conflict, and rejection.

The rules up the ante on this vulnerability, though, especially if you've learned to attach your worth to avoiding criticism, conflict, and rejection. It's vulnerable to say no and set boundaries when you've always been the yes person everyone likes. It's vulnerable to challenge a comment, policy, or practice when you've been valued for keeping the peace and going with the flow. It's vulnerable to share a brand-new idea that might not be right when you're the person who always gets it right. It's vulnerable to start doing something "weird" your family might not understand when you've always been the easy, low-maintenance kid among your siblings and cousins. It's vulnerable to share your truth with a partner when you've been smiling, nodding, and ignoring that truth for many years.

The bottom line is, it's vulnerable to break the rules when you've been taught that your worth lies in conforming to them. And yet, it's worth it.

It's vulnerable to break the rules and take up space. But it's worse to keep yourself hidden.

How Do You Take up Space?

There's no deep reflection exercise here. Learning to take up space comes down to one word: PRACTICE. Remind yourself of your "I am a person who . . ." declarations. Lean into vulnerability and discomfort, and make an active choice to show up as that person in the world. Put yourself out there, time and time again.

It's a continual practice for me as well.

My first book, *An Overachiever's Guide to Breaking the Rules*, has been recognized with four awards. The first two were both under the umbrella of the Eric Hoffer Book Awards and arrived together. I was honored and excited to receive them—and perfectly happy to share them with everyone else too!

Just a few weeks later, the book won a Next Generation Indie Book Award. I was overwhelmed in the best way possible. I told my parents and a few close friends without any apprehension. When I thought about sharing the award with a broader audience, however, the fear of arrogance

I described at the beginning of the chapter swooped in hard. It filled me with dread at the thought of posting about the book award on social media. I felt like telling people was saying, "Hey, look at me! Aren't I awesome?!"

The anxiety was big enough that it took me a few weeks to get up the motivation to tell everyone about the award. At the same time, I recognized this feeling as the discomfort of moving into a bigger space and the rules telling me to quiet my voice and hide my accomplishments. Because I am a woman who breaks the rules with purpose and lives in my fullness without apology, though, I knew I had to take action. So I wrote a blurb for social media and hit Post. My heart thumped in my chest, and a nervous pit sat in my stomach, but I hit the button anyway.

You know what happened? None of my fears came true. Instead, people were EXCITED—and that made *me* excited! If there were people who thought it was arrogant or too much, they certainly didn't voice it. It shouldn't matter anyway. I had earned that award, and I had a right to be proud of it.*

Putting yourself out there in a large, public way isn't the only way to practice taking up space. Sometimes taking up space is simply sharing the truths you've hidden with one person— and feeling the freedom that comes from letting that truth see the light of day.

I recently dated a guy for a few months. I'd like to say that I showed up in grounded wildness 100 percent of the time,

---

* *An Overachiever's Guide to Breaking the Rules* has since been honored with a Living Now Book Award as well.

but that wasn't the truth. For years, I had hidden from any guy with dating potential the fact that I'd never had a serious relationship, and this guy was no different. I was worried about his reaction and anticipated judgment for my lack of relationship experience. I was afraid he would think something must be wrong with me that he just hadn't seen yet. I had released most of my shame in this arena, but pieces of it were still lurking, hiding in deep crevasses.

One day, we played a game where we could ask each other any questions we wanted for five minutes, and he asked me about the last time I was in a serious relationship. A huge lump swelled in my throat—a physical sign of the shame telling me to keep quiet. At the same time, I wasn't going to lie. I could evade a subject like a pro, but I've never been good at lying when asked a direct question.

I took a deep breath and said, "I've never been in a serious relationship."

The guy was taken aback. His whole face transformed into surprise. It wasn't negative exactly, but it was a strong reaction.

And I survived it. I said the truth that had caused me so much worry over the years. With that admission, a few more of the dark crevasses of shame turned to light.

This might not sound like an example of taking up space. I wasn't on stage. I wasn't challenging authority. I wasn't publishing a book or sending an email to 1,000 people. Instead, I was taking up space by speaking my truth. I revealed parts of myself I had done my best to keep hidden for decades. I stood in my grounded wildness—which told me I was already whole, worthy, and complete—and said (albeit nervously),

"This is my truth. Take it or leave it."

In that moment, I was free.

I practiced again. The next guy I dated reacted with complete neutrality, like I was saying something important but without any judgment attached to it. If anything, there was compassion. That affirmation may have dissolved the shame forever.

Over time, you'll notice that taking up space and sharing your hard truths, power, and radiance gets easier. The freedom that comes with living as your full self in the world overtakes the fear of possible rejection and criticism. You'll learn it's harder to perform and hide yourself than it is to let yourself loose.

Every time I take up the space of my full self, I let go of another thread of performing. Allowing others to see my radiance allows me to believe it for myself on a deeper level. I feel free in my wholeness because I am letting the whole of me out into the world.

In the midst of my second big break, as I was stepping into larger spaces daily, I wrote this in my journal: "I am starting to live with my spirit loose. It's starting to break free and my soul—my true inner voice—is whispering: *Keep going, keep going. Soon, you will be flying.*"

Now I say those same words to you. Embrace the discomfort. Lean into the newfound freedom you are experiencing. Keep going, keep going. Soon, you will be flying.

CHAPTER 20

Not Everyone Will Get It—and That's Okay

When I left my stable corporate job to start my own business, I wondered if people would think I was foolish. Leaving a company for a great opportunity elsewhere was one thing. Leaving behind an entire career where I was on a path to continued "success" was a completely different scenario. I was confident it was the right decision for me, but I had no idea how others would react.

When I put in my notice and announced my decision to friends, family, and colleagues, I discovered most of my fears surrounding the question "What will they think?" were unfounded. Most people were supportive. Shockingly supportive.

What surprised me most was the number of people who quietly and privately told me they'd considered doing the same thing. They let me know in hushed tones that starting their own business was sitting in the back of their mind as a "someday" goal.

This wasn't everyone, though. There was another group of people who were a little more skeptical of my plans.

None of these people told me directly, "Heather, this is a stupid idea. You shouldn't do this." For that, I feel lucky. I know that not everyone is so fortunate when they make the seemingly illogical decision to upend their career— or any other big decision that takes you off the standard, expected path.

Some people just didn't get it, however. These were people I cared about and who cared about me. They weren't directly unsupportive, but it was clear they didn't understand why I would do such a thing.

I got a similar response when I moved to Colorado. Most people were supportive. They understood how much I loved to hike and adventure, and they saw that this was a great move for me. Same as before, several people told me they had also considered packing up and making a big move for no particularly logical or "good" reason.

The flip side happened again as well. Some people saw the incredible support network I had in Minnesota and wondered why I would start over in a new place where

I only knew a few people. They questioned why I would move in the middle of a global pandemic, when it would be even harder to make new friends. They brought up the difference in the cost of housing and let me know just how expensive it would be to live in Colorado.

This is happening again as I write this book. Most people think it's amazing that I'm writing a second book. I've also had people tell me directly that there's no reason to write another book yet. I have plenty of mileage left out of the first one. People love my speaking topics. Why introduce something new that could upset the positive business trajectory I have going?

In all these situations, there have been supportive people who understand what I'm doing—and there have been others who don't get it. And that's completely, totally, 100 percent okay. It's my life. Not theirs. They don't have to get it. Only I need to get it.

The same is true for your life as well.

Not only is it okay if people don't get it, but it's also okay if they actively don't like it. It's okay if they disagree with your decisions. It's okay if you unequivocally disappoint them.

Most of these reactions come from a place of caring. The people in your life want you to be safe. They want you to be protected from potential failure, hurt, rejection, and criticism (even though they may be criticizing you in the process—the irony!). What's more, they were also handed a set of rules like you were, and seeing you break those rules may make them deeply uncomfortable. They might not get your rule-breaking grounded wildness, but they aren't getting it from a place of love.

There's another group out there as well. These people are threatened by you living in grounded wildness. When you stop performing, you become a changemaker. You stop following the path that maintains the status quo and start following your own path. You ask hard questions and challenge power structures. A woman breaking the rules in her own life is a threat to the rules everywhere.

There are risks with both groups. Your parents may be disappointed if you jump ship from the career they expected to pursue what you really want. Your entire family may be upset if you forgo the Christmas vacation you've taken with them for the last ten years to go on your dream trip to Costa Rica. They may be a whole other level of disappointed if you decide not to have children, thus denying them the opportunity to be grandparents, cousins, aunts, and uncles.

This goes for work as well. Your boss may get angry if you challenge senior leaders at your company. Your team may get frustrated if you don't check your emails while you're on vacation if everyone else checks theirs on their out-of-office time. You may get feedback to watch your tone if you speak up. Those actions might affect your performance review.

The risks are real, particularly if you are challenging power and authority. The more identities you have that aren't white, cisgender, straight, and male, the greater those risks become.

I've also found, however, that the potential consequences usually feel bigger in my head than how they end up in real life. You make a decision, speak up, disagree, or set a boundary—and it's fine. Perhaps you get a question or two, but people don't care nearly as much as you worry they will.

Only you can decide what's worth the risk. Only you can determine what's worth people not getting it, not liking it, being disappointed by it, or disagreeing with it. Only you can decide what is worth the potential criticism.

You are the only person who can determine what it's worth to stop performing your life and start living it. Not the life expected of you. Not the life prescribed for you. Your life. Your truth. Your version of Sweet Girl and Fire, both alive in the world. All of you, separate from the rules you've been handed, living in grounded wildness.

How do you do that? How do you figure out what's worth it? How do you respond to the people who just don't get it? Or who actively discourage you from following your grounded wildness? All the practices we've talked about in this book will help. Creating space to hear your knowing, following what makes you come alive, and claiming yourself will all guide you to reconnect to *you*—and disconnect you from the thoughts and opinions of those who don't get it.

Here are two additional suggestions, which you'll read in the rest of this chapter:

1. Determine the consequence you want less.
2. Set boundaries.

Determine the Consequence You Want Less

One of my coaching clients, Amy, recently scheduled a two-week vacation. She planned to disconnect entirely and give herself the opportunity to recharge. Amy loved her work, but she was on the verge of burnout and needed a break.

Here's the catch, though: No one at her leadership level on her team had ever taken a two-week vacation. Ever.

Amy knew that checking out for two weeks might disappoint her team members. She also knew her external clients might not like it. Even though she put backup plans in place, she knew they might all prefer for her to be available (at least occasionally) during those two weeks.

So Amy asked herself, "Which consequence do I want less?"

One side of the coin was the potential to disappoint people. On the other side of the coin were the consequences of NOT getting a full break, namely returning to work and life still stressed and on the verge of burnout.

In the end, Amy decided that she preferred the potential consequence of disappointing people to continued stress and burnout. You can do the same by asking yourself questions to determine which consequence *you* want less. For example:

- Do you prefer the discomfort of saying no? Or the resentment of having said yes?
- Do you prefer having the hard conversation with your family member regarding the jokes they make about your past mistakes at every family gathering? Or the continued exasperation of smiling through those jokes and pretending everything is fine while you're curdling inside with anger and embarrassment?
- Do you prefer the potential questions you may get (and not know the answer to) when you share

a new idea? Or keeping your idea locked away, never to impact anyone?

- Do you prefer to disappoint your wonderful manager, who is grooming you to take over their role? Or staying in a job that makes you want to get up and RUN out of the office every day?
- Do you prefer sharing your voice and being called direct? Or enduring the façade of tucking yourself in and holding back your voice?
- Do you prefer living YOUR life? Or continuing to perform to keep others happy and comfortable?

There's always a choice. What do you choose?

Set Boundaries

What do you do with people who don't get it, don't approve of it, or don't like it—and they're vocal about it?

For example, you walk into a coffee date with a friend feeling solid in your knowing, then walk out two hours later caffeinated and questioning everything you were certain about just a few hours earlier. Or, maybe you know something big needs to change in your job, but every time you meet with your mentor, they convince you that you're already on the right path and there's no need for change. Or, maybe you feel grounded in how you want to run your business, but every time you log onto social media, you're blasted with ads telling you how to build a seven-figure business, and you see photos of people in your industry who are seemingly way more successful than you, and you feel . . . behind.*

I have one answer for you: set boundaries.

There are a lot of definitions of boundaries out there, but I personally like this simple one the best: boundaries are what's okay with you and what's not.

This means you get to decide if you're okay with continuing to tolerate the friend who makes you question your knowing, the mentor who derails your career aspirations, and the social media blasting unhelpful messages in your face. You get to decide all of that.

Sometimes extreme boundaries are needed, like cutting a toxic person out of your life. Most of the time, though, boundaries look more like a statement of your needs:

- To the friend: "I appreciate your concern, but I know this is the right decision for me. It's hard for me to say this because I value your opinion, but I don't need your input here. I'd like your support, but that's all I need."

- To the mentor: "I know you want what's best for me, and I appreciate your belief in my ability to be successful on this career path. But I need to go a different route. I need you to stop questioning my decision."

- To social media: Okay, this isn't an actual conversation (although you can have one in your head, if you like!), but you can set boundaries about which platforms you're on, how many, and how often. I'm working on this area myself, because some aspects of social

---

* This last one definitely happens to me on occasion.

media are beneficial for my business and connecting with friends and family . . . and there are tolls on my attention, time, and the aforementioned feeling of being behind.

One action has been a game-changer for me in this realm: Unfollow those who make you feel behind in a game you don't want to play. One day, I sat down and literally unfollowed, unconnected, and even unfriended every person whose posts made me feel like I should be working harder, doing more, or striving for a business and life I didn't actually want. Their posts drew me back to the rules I'd been taught and tempted me to believe I had to prove, please, and perfect to be "successful." They pulled me away from my grounded wildness.

I knew some of these people personally. I had hired others as coaches and consultants for my business in the past. They weren't bad people; I just didn't need to see their posts. And I had no obligation to keep doing so.

You don't, either. You can have the hard conversation and lay down the boundary of what's okay with you and what's not. You can expend less energy on people who don't make you feel good, even if you've known them for twenty years. You get to decide how you spend your time and who you spend it with.

You get to decide.

A Final Note about People Not Getting It

An interesting thing has happened to me as I've stepped more and more into grounded wildness: I care less about whether people get it or not.

I can't say that I care *zero*, and I don't think that's the goal. But there's been a noticeable trajectory of disconnecting my decisions from other people's opinions about them.

Breaking free from performing my life and stepping into grounded wildness has become a reinforcing cycle. The more I follow my own knowing, the better it feels. I'm freer and more alive. I have deeper relationships. My work makes a bigger difference. I continually want more of everything grounded wildness has to offer.

The opposite has also been true. When I've gotten sucked back into proving, pleasing, and perfecting, I end up stressed, overcommitted, and exhausted. When I ignore my knowing, it feels terrible. I wind up living a life I never wanted. People might understand that life better. It might be more "normal." But it's not my life. And I always want to live *my* life.

You'll find this as well. It will likely be uncomfortable when you stop performing. You'll probably worry about what people will think. You might not know how to have conversations with the people who don't get it, don't like it, or don't approve of it.

Over time, though, you'll find yourself untethered from the need for their validation. You'll be open to feedback and new perspectives, but the "I don't get it" and "I don't like it" reactions will matter less and less. You'll recognize that praise feels good, but it's not required for your self-worth.

You'll realize you can care about people without caring about every opinion they have on your life.

You'll see that YOU get it. And that's all that matters.

CHAPTER 21

Find Your Grounded Wildness Community

A few years ago, I attended a conference with two good friends. During a break, the three of us went outside to escape the darkness of the windowless hotel ballroom and rejuvenate ourselves with fresh air and sunshine. While we were chatting, a sudden breeze came up, and one of my friends grabbed her wrap dress unusually tight—and then confided she wasn't wearing any underwear.

My third friend and I were awestruck. It hadn't occurred to either of us that we had the option to forgo underwear out in public. Especially at a professional event. Especially in a DRESS!

"No wonder you always look so free!" my other friend exclaimed to her with admiration.

It became a running joke between us. I texted this friend on the first day I opted to shed my underwear, with this message: "Everyone needs a friend they can tell when they choose to go pantyless for the first time."

A few months later, she texted us again, telling us she had attended the first day of a training while wearing her underwear and had decided to ditch it for the second day of training. She wrote, "Today I am FREE. And I feel so good."

Then she texted something I'll never forget: "I'm so grateful to be in a friendship with two women who hold space for me to feel free in my own ways."

In the previous chapter, we talked about the people who don't get it. This chapter is all about the people who DO. This is your grounded wildness community.

They are the people who hold space for your freedom. They encourage your wildness. They sit with you while you're feeling your feelings. They stand alongside you, seeking aliveness. They encourage you to follow your knowing, even when it doesn't make sense to them. They give you the space to fully claim yourself, take up space, and live into your truth.

You never have to perform for your grounded wildness community. You don't have to drink to be more fun for them. You don't have to dress a certain way to avoid judging looks. You don't have to clean your house before they come over. You don't have to smile and pretend everything is fine when it's not. You don't have to prove yourself to them by getting the promotion, but they'll sit with you in disappointment when you don't get it and celebrate big with you when you do. They don't care if you meditate every day or serve organic kale to your five-year-old. They don't care if you're a complete and total mess with grief or putting on a public display of ecstasy, joy, and wonder.

You can never be too much for your grounded wildness community. Or too little. They see your radiance and reflect a mirror on you to shine even brighter. They're there with you in your light—and in your dark.

In chapter 14, Feel Your Feelings, I mentioned that I'd been pretty terrible at exactly that for most of my life. It's been a journey to learn how to feel my feelings without judgment and allow them to flow through me. It's been an even bigger journey to do that in front of other people.

Instead of calling a friend when I was in the throes of big emotions, I'd cry on my own. Wallow solo with wine, ice cream, and the Hallmark Channel. Sob within the safe confines of my condo.

Then I'd talk to my friends. I'd share the hard feelings in a way that was distanced once I was past the biggest part of the mess and could discuss my emotions rationally. I'd intellectualize my feelings without letting go and showing their physical manifestation. No tears, just words.

I would occasionally break down in front of other people, but those moments were few and far between—and never by choice. I did everything I could to hold in tears, shaking, puffy eyes, and a running nose, even around people I trusted deeply.

Then my second big break happened.

At that moment, I needed the support of other humans, and there was no possible way to control my emotions. They were overflowing from every orifice of my being. I was either going to suffer alone or let myself be seen in all my mess. I chose the latter.

I called a good friend and sobbed into the phone for over an hour. There were times during the conversation when my tears came so hard that I found myself gasping for breath, trying to get out words that I'm sure sounded like a wreckage of incoherence on the other end.

My friend was there for all of it, though. She listened. She occasionally reflected back things I had said. She validated that this was hard, and that my feelings were normal.

More than anything, though, my friend witnessed. She saw all my big feelings. She didn't try to reason with them. She didn't try to squash them down. She didn't try to make them pretty or tie anything in a bow. Instead, she created an environment where I could find freedom in allowing my feelings to flow. Nothing held back, I could let it all show. It was exactly what I needed.

You need this, too. Not just during your big breaks, or during other times when grief strikes and challenging emotions overwhelm you. You also need your grounded wildness community when:

- You decide to have a discussion with your boss about how they continually interrupt the women on your team—and it doesn't go well.
- You need to go out of town for a fun girls' weekend.

- You won a big award at work, and you want to celebrate and bask in all your glory.
- You're contemplating divorce from the partner you've been married to for twenty years, and you can't find your footing.
- You want to have a *real* conversation. No pretend smiling. No fake emotions. You want to get to the heart of the matter—whatever it may be—right away.
- You made an offer on a house, and you're simultaneously excited and nervous—and you need to meet someone for a cocktail who will cheers to your excitement *and* listen to your nerves.

In a world that will tell you to cut off your wildness and go back to performing, you need your people to encourage, support, and hold your freedom. They need the same from you. We aren't meant to do this alone.

Let's get started with building your community.

Who Already Holds Space for Your Freedom?

You may already have people in your grounded wildness community without even knowing it. If you aren't sure, think about all your people and answer these questions:

- Who do you feel free around?
- Who requires zero performing from you? No proving, pleasing, perfecting, or rebelling needed for you to feel accepted?
- Who encourages you to follow *your* path, as opposed to what *they* think is right for you?

Who comes up when you reflect on these questions? It could be the group of girlfriends you've known forever who always understand you without any explanation needed. It could be the friend you met six months ago who helps you uncover new insights about yourself every time you hang out with them. It could be the colleague who cheerleads you into applying for the new job you really want, even though you aren't sure you're ready. It could be the cousin who's so in tune with herself that she walks through the world with freedom, inspiring you to do the same.

Your grounded wildness community doesn't need to be all women, but I've found it's vital to have women in my life who live into their freedom and encourage mine. Other women understand all the proving, pleasing, and perfecting rules that have been handed down to you. They know the challenges of breaking those rules and making up their own game.

As I move further into my own grounded wildness journey, I find myself drawn to spending more time with these women. When I'm feeling behind in my business and edging toward the slippery slope of hustle culture, they remind me I'm not on any timeline. They cheered with me when I won my first book award. They listened without judgment when I disclosed the vision I have for sharing the messages of this book on big stages. They believed it was possible right along with me.

They're also there to hop in a car without any plans and spend a day driving in the mountains, searching for golden aspen in the fall. They tell me it's fine (or not just fine, but amazing!) to go kayaking in Mexico for a week without checking a single email. They talk me through a guy I'm dating, share their experiences, and ask questions to help me find the right way forward for me.

They lead by example, give me permission, and hold space for my freedom. They remind me of who I am.

Who does that for you?

Who Do You Need?

The first time I ever attended a Unitarian Universalist (UU) church was on Zoom in January 2021, during the dark winter days of the pandemic. I'd always been curious about UU, but I had never looked into what they were about because I'd been a part of a wonderful spiritual community in Minneapolis that fulfilled my needs.

Moving to Colorado meant leaving that spiritual community behind—and it left open gaps that needed to be filled in my life. Knowing this, a good friend in Minnesota reached out to me, suggesting I check out Foothills Unitarian Universalist Church, where she knew one of the ministers.

I decided to take her advice. I logged onto Zoom at 9:00 a.m. the following Sunday with the intention of listening to the service and then participating in small-group breakout rooms.

The service hit me unexpectedly hard. It dove deep into racism and white supremacy and showed images of the uprisings following the murders of George Floyd, Breonna Taylor, and many others. Grief and rage rose inside me with startling power. I sat in my apartment with my video turned off, shaking and sobbing throughout the service.

I attempted to pull myself together enough to go into the breakout room after the service ended. I was craving human connection, even if that was just over Zoom with a bunch of people I'd never met. I shoved down my tears, took a breath, and joined the breakout room.

As soon as I got there, the crying started again. There I was, on camera, with five strangers, attending a totally new church in a religion I knew nothing about. And I was a bawling mess.

The facilitator asked the first discussion question. One by one, everyone responded, until it was just me left to share. I figured I better say something so that they weren't sitting there waiting for me. I took a breath, clicked Unmute, and choked out through active tears that I was having a hard time and would probably just listen.

Here was the immediate response from one of the breakout group members: "That's completely fine. My mom always said, 'If you can't cry in church, where can you cry?'"

Tears are coming to my eyes right now as I write this, remembering that response. In a single sentence, this woman gave me permission to show up exactly as I was. There was no discomfort with my emotion. No one suggested I leave or turn off my video and collect myself. I didn't have to perform a single thing.

In that moment, I thought, *This is exactly what I've been looking for. I have found my people.*

A year and a half later, as I write this book, this UU church is still my people. They hold space for my freedom in a different way than the individual women in my life, but in a way that is just as important. They challenge me without telling me what to think or believe. They remind me of what's important, for me in my life and for our world as a whole. They show me time and time again how to see and feel hard things while also experiencing deep wonder, joy, and gratitude.

This isn't an advertisement for UU churches. Mine just happened to fulfill a gap I had in my life for a community that upholds my grounded wildness. This is about taking a step back for yourself and determining what *you* need in *your* grounded wildness community.

Pause and ask yourself right now, "Where is my grounded wildness community going strong? Where do I have gaps?"

For example, you may have a group of friends who are fun, free, and always there for spontaneity and aliveness. You love this. You also know they aren't the best when it comes to the serious stuff. This is a gap.

Once you've identified where your community is going strong and where you have gaps, brainstorm a few actions to keep your current relationships fed and fill the holes in your grounded wildness community.

I recently realized I had a gap in my life when it came to play. I wasn't sure how to fill this need, so one day I quite literally Googled "Fun classes for adults near me." The very first search result was an event called Let's Dance Outside Together. I liked that title!

I clicked on the event description and signed up. Three days later, I found myself on the outskirts of town, walking through one of the most beautiful gardens I'd ever seen. The garden led to an open grassy space underneath a towering cottonwood tree that must have been hundreds of years old. The whole thing overlooked the entire panorama of the Rocky Mountains from north to south.

Over the next two hours, we (me and the other people participating in Let's Dance Outside Together) each shared deeply with a partner, wandered the garden, lay still on our blankets, and then *danced*. Our instructor reminded us to let go of any shoulds and follow our bodies. There were no required steps. We could move slowly. Or dance big. Or just lie on our blankets the entire time.

This class fulfilled exactly what I needed. I went back again two weeks later. And a few weeks after that. And a few weeks after that.

The people who showed up for Let's Dance Outside Together weren't my best friends. I never saw some of them again after that first meeting, but they created an environment of play and release for me—and I contributed to creating that environment for them. They held space for my freedom for those two hours. They filled a gap in my grounded wildness community so quickly that it overflowed.

There is no right or wrong way to fulfill your needs. Maybe Google will give you the answers too! Maybe you'll need to ask people how they've fulfilled the gaps you've identified. Maybe your needs can be met through a class or experience— or maybe you need to build relationships over time.

You can also look to strangers for inspiration. I've always said that Elizabeth Gilbert, Brené Brown, and Maya Angelou are my trio of mentors I've never actually met (outside of being an audience member at their events!). When I need a reminder of my grounded wildness, I look back on the ways they've inspired me.

I remember how Elizabeth Gilbert told a packed audience at the Paramount Theatre in Denver that she was seeking to be a *relaxed* woman—and how I immediately dropped further into my own relaxation when she said those words. That's some grounded wildness energy right there.

I also remember watching Brené Brown's Netflix special, *The Call to Courage*, two days before getting on stage at my biggest speaking engagement to date. I turned it on to observe how she carried her body on stage and learn from her presentation skills. While that was helpful, what I really needed in that moment was the deep reminder that it's not the critic who counts. I needed someone to show me that I could get on that stage exactly as I am and take my spot in the arena. That's all grounded wildness.

Finally, I remember the joyful freedom of Maya Angelou's laugh the one time I saw her in person. She was sitting on stage, already in her eighties, and absolutely cracked herself up with one of the stories she was going to share—before she could even get the words out to the rest of us! She was free to enjoy her own joy. Serious grounded wildness.

Now, it's your turn. Find the people, communities, and experiences that inspire you and remind you of your grounded wildness. Take a chance and show up at an event. Reach out to someone you'd like to develop a deeper relationship with. It may be uncomfortable to walk into that class alone. It may feel awkward asking someone out on a "friend date." But that's okay. I promise that you will live through the awkwardness. If you find kinship and freedom, the discomfort will melt away quickly. If you hate it, you never have to go back to that class or hang out with that person again. It's a worthwhile risk.

Be a Haven for Grounded Wildness

Most of this chapter has been about finding the people who encourage *your* grounded wildness. This may go without saying, but it's a two-way street: Your grounded wildness community holds space for your freedom—and you hold space for theirs.

Being a haven for grounded wildness goes beyond your close friends and individual relationships. You encourage grounded wildness in others every time you do any of the following:

- Allow someone to feel their feelings, no matter what they are (assuming they are expressing those emotions in a way that doesn't hurt you or others, of course).
- Ask someone, "What feels right to you?" instead of chiming in with what *you* think is right for *them*.
- Tell people with your words or actions that they are welcome to show up exactly as they are, no performing needed.
- Share something vulnerable about yourself, thereby giving them permission to do the same.
- Call out microaggressions that shut people down, and use your privilege to advocate for others who are sharing ideas and challenging the status quo.
- Create space to question and discuss the rules you've been handed.

There are a million ways you can hold space for someone's freedom. The main criterion is that you detach yourself from their outcomes. It's their journey, not yours. It's not your responsibility to force someone into a break or convince them they need to change their life and start living in grounded wildness.

Your job is to believe in their radiance and shine a light on the path they are walking, even if that path looks completely different from what you imagined. There is no greater gift than reminding someone of who they are and holding space for them to grow into themselves and find their freedom.

You do it for them, and they do it for you. You stay grounded, wild, and free *together*.

CHAPTER 22

The Journey Continues

scrapped 90 percent of this final chapter between the first and second drafts of this book. Some of that was part of the normal editing process. I *really* embrace the idea of "shitty first drafts" from Anne Lamott, so that approach always leads to a decent number of updates—and a significantly less shitty second draft!

This chapter was different, though. When I read through the first draft, it felt too factual. It stayed too close to the surface. It sounded like grounded wildness, but it didn't quite *feel* like grounded wildness. Deep changes were needed to bring the book together and send you on your journey.

Why? Because *my* journey into grounded wildness had to continue before I could write the final chapter of this book. I had to dive deeper. Practice more. *Live* more.

I will keep diving deeper as I travel through the coming months and years. I will discover more of myself. I will get more grounded and wild with every step forward.

My journey will continue, every day, for the rest of my life. So will yours.

The last chapter of *An Overachiever's Guide to Breaking the Rules* is also titled "The Journey Continues." It wouldn't surprise me if the next book I write will also finish with "The Journey Continues."

I can think of no better message to send at the end of a personal development book. Life is not a check-the-box activity. Your journey toward grounded wildness began long before you started reading this book, and it will continue forever. It is an ongoing process of *letting go* and *becoming*.

I recently saw a social media post that said something like, "Cheers to not knowing who you are because you've stopped pretending to be someone you're not." This is letting go.

You might be here right now. You've become aware of the rules you were handed. You see how proving, pleasing, perfecting, and rebelling have shown up in your life. You understand how performing has taken you away from yourself.

You know where you lost your *youthful* wildness, but you may not have claimed your *grounded* wildness. That is normal, understandable, and completely okay.

There's a continuum from performing to living in grounded wildness. It's not an overnight journey. It's not something that happens automatically from reading this book (or even from writing it!).

It's in the big breaks and the million messy steps in between. It's in the rules you notice and challenge. It's you catching yourself in performance mode and gently recalibrating so that you can settle into grounded wildness again. It's in learning a new way of living.

The two breaks I described in this book accelerated my journey from performing to grounded wildness in huge ways. They broke me down, open, and through—hard and fast, especially the second one. That break went far beyond men, dating, and realizing my radiance. It seeped into all areas of my life and launched me into a freedom I didn't know was possible. I understood how it felt to be both grounded and wild for the first time in my life.

My journey toward grounded wildness has been more than these two breaks, however. It's been a multiyear process of letting go of proving, pleasing, perfecting, and rebelling so that I have the space to become who I am.

The letting go happens first, then the becoming. Neither is a linear, point-A-to-point-B process. You will turn, plummet, and soar. You will let go and become, then let go and become again, over and over and over.

I am in yet another moment of becoming as I write this chapter.

A few months ago, I began sensing a shift in myself. I felt like I was on the precipice of something big, but I couldn't articulate what it was. I was standing on the edge of a mountain, wanting to fly, but I didn't know how to unfurl my wings, take the leap, and soar.

So I hired a coach. Through working with this coach, I realized how much more I can still sink into grounded wildness. I knew grounded wildness in my head. I felt it in my heart. Now I'm learning to live from it in my *body*.

I'd (mostly) released the proving, pleasing, and perfecting rules from an intellectual level. My brain knew I had nothing to prove. I believed I was radiant, whole, and complete, deeply in my heart.

Part of my body, on the other hand, was stuck in performing mode. I'd already come a long way with reconnecting with my body and letting it lead. It didn't operate in the same way as it had during my hardcore overachieving years. I raced around in manic mode far less often. I relaxed more easily. The pit in my stomach showed up much less frequently.

My body wasn't living in grounded wildness, though— and I didn't even know it until I started working with this coach. Through our sessions, she guided me to notice the tightness in my pelvis and then breathe to relax and ground in that power center of my body. She helped me realize how often I am leaning forward, practically leaping out of my chair with proving, pleasing, and perfecting energy. She guided me to lean back and trust the support behind me, in both tangible and metaphorical ways.

What's more, she helped me unlock a greater permission to speak, work, and live from my fire even more than I had already been doing. I've begun sharing my story more directly on stage. I've started challenging bias more than I used to. I worry less about being polite and more about speaking the truth, in both my work and my personal life.

Every day, I am living more into the woman I am. A woman who challenges the status quo, breaks the rules *with* purpose, and lives in her fullness without apology. A woman who is truly free and alive.

I knew I was on the precipice of something big. What I didn't know was that the something big turned out to be me.

The threshold I felt inside me wasn't about the next big thing to accomplish. It wasn't about stages, recognition, or publishing this book. It was about living my truth. My *full* truth. Uncaging Fire. Unfurling my wings, stretching them wide, and taking flight.

You will have your own versions of letting go and becoming as well. Your own thresholds of growth that will allow you to release the next weight of performing, unfurl your wings a little wider, and take flight.

Old rules will also reappear. A large portion of the world will try to pull you back into performing. You will get direct and indirect messages telling you to play the role you've been given, confine yourself back to the box, and shut the lid.

When that happens, come back to yourself. Reconnect to your aliveness. Feel the fire burning deep within, and fan the flames. And remember exactly who you are.

You are enough, worthy, and whole.

You belong within.

You are *radiant*.

And you get to make up your own rules for life.

Then bring in the reinforcements: your grounded wildness community. Together, you will encourage one another's freedom. Their presence will fortify your strength. You will do the same for them.

Your grounded wildness will spread to other women. It may make some people uncomfortable, but others will be in awe. They will be attracted to your energy and want to live in the same freedom. They will start questioning the rules they've been handed and create their own rules for life.

Our individual breaks will crash together into collective breaks. The shame of nonconformity will blossom into the freedom of nonconformity. This is when systems and structures break down. This is when power transfers from the few to the many. This is change.

But I don't want you to worry about all that right now. Today, I want you to read the words I wrote in the midst of my second big break, when I was on the verge of emerging into grounded wildness:

> Start now. There is no need to wait for anything. Start being the person you want to be now. Start being the person you already are. RIGHT NOW. You don't have to fit yourself into the box of what you think is acceptable. GET OUT OF THE BOX. You never belonged in it anyway. Take a risk. A real chance. Be free. Be free. Love, love, love with everything you are. Surrender. Let go. Stop playing by the rules. Live free, be free, do all things free. LIVE YOUR TRUTH. Be all of it. And start now.

ABOUT THE AUTHOR

Heather Whelpley is an award-winning author, speaker, and the podcast host of *Grounded Wildness*. She leads presentations and workshops at companies and conferences on creating your own rules for success, imposter syndrome, and discovering your authentic voice and how to use it to create change.

Heather has spoken to thousands of people across the US and internationally, including Fortune 500 companies, nonprofits, universities, and associations. Prior to starting her business, Heather spent over a decade in human resources and managing development programs for high-achieving women at Fortune 500 companies in the US, Australia, and Latin America.

Her first book, *An Overachiever's Guide to Breaking the Rules: How to Let Go of Perfect and Live Your Truth*, has won multiple awards, including the Next Generation Indie Book Awards, Living Now Book Awards, and the Eric Hoffer Book Awards. Today, Heather lives in Colorado where she spends as much time hiking and exploring as possible.

Listen to the *Grounded Wildness* podcast, read Heather's blog, and learn more about booking her as a speaker at www.heatherwhelpley.com.

ACKNOWLEDGMENTS

My journey to grounded wildness was deeply personal, but it wasn't a journey I walked alone. So many people contributed to that journey—and to publishing this book.

First and foremost, to my grounded wildness community. You've been there through uncontrollable tears—and uncontrollable laughter. You've jumped in a car and driven down a dirt road in the mountains just to see what we might find. You've listened and asked questions and reflected my own truth back to me. I don't know where I'd be without you.

To my mom, who never said the words "grounded wildness community," but who showed me the importance of having women friends in your life who could be there with you through all of life's experiences. And who always encouraged me to follow my heart and believed all my dreams were possible.

To all the people who listened and got excited with me when I talked through the concept of grounded wildness, especially LJ, Alix, Betsy, Monica, Sarah, Courtney, and Amy. I love that most of our conversations about grounded wildness also took place on hiking trails. We got grounded and wild as we talked about grounded wildness!

To my four beta readers, Nikki, Brenna, Lauren, and Michele, who gave their time and energy to read every word of this book and provide feedback. They were also the first people to read *Grounded Wildness* and were able to hold the vulnerability that came along with that. This book is immensely better because of you.

To Jess Morphew, who captured the heart of grounded wildness with her design for the cover of this book—and who patiently created multiple versions of the word "Wildness" until it was just right!

To the entire team at Wise Ink Creative Publishing and especially to Dara Beevas, who embodies grounded wildness and reminded me to follow my own grounded wildness when making decisions about this book.

And, finally, to you. Thank you for taking a chance on this book—and on yourself. Thank you for diving in deep, exploring the rules you were handed, and allowing your own glimpses of wildness to come to the surface. Thank you for reading *Grounded Wildness* and sharing it with the women in your life.

This book is for all of us. A grounded wildness community of women breaking free and creating our own rules for life.

SPEAKING & BOOK ENDORSEMENTS
FOR Grounded Wildness

"*Grounded Wildness* provides valuable insight on forgiving yourself for the ways we as women have been conditioned to prove, please, perfect, and perform as well as how we can forge our own unique path forward. Heather's vulnerability in sharing her experiences provides the perfect backdrop for taking a critical look at the way we treat ourselves, and the treatment we accept from those around us. Don't shy away from doing the work Heather lays out in this book—feel your feelings and find your community! You're sure to come out better for it on the other side.

I've also hired Heather for several speaking engagements and it is always an absolute joy to work with her! Anyone thinking of engaging her as a speaker should absolutely do it. Heather is exceptionally well organized, thorough in her questions and review, and can tailor the experience to your organization. I would bring her on for another speaking engagement in a heartbeat!"

—JESSICA SARES, ITW Women's Network
Global Events co-chair

(CONTINUED)

"*Grounded Wildness* is utterly honest and vulnerable. The question, '*Does Heather know she is beautiful?*' strikes at the core of so many of our insecurities. Heather compels the reader to urgently find their true self while providing a playbook for how to start. A must read for anyone looking for greater fulfillment out of life.

Additionally, Heather spoke at our company and was dynamic, engaging, authentic, and created a space where our employees felt comfortable sharing and engaging on topics previously 'off limits' with colleagues. It was incredible to see the vulnerability our employees shared BECAUSE of the brave and open space Heather immediately created with the group. What's more, in our post-event survey, 100 percent of employees said they plan to use the tools from the session in their ongoing development!"

—SARAH STREHL, chief human resources officer, ECMC Group

"Heather writes so honestly and speaks to audiences in the same way—from the very place of grounded wildness she talks about. This book gives shape to things we don't normally notice and shines light onto that which we don't question, but holds us back. Through speaking her own story, Heather provides the opportunity for us each to find the path to our own grounded wildness."

—MONICA SMITH, managing director, Talent and Diversity, Equity, and Inclusion, The Toro Company

"After years of performing, *Grounded Wildness* made me stop and think about how I got there. I do so many things mentioned in this book so frequently it has become who I am. I realized I need to break some of those rules to find myself—and please myself. I particularly connected with the question, 'Do I prefer truly living my life—or performing to keep others happy and comfortable?' Heather's vulnerability in this book is inspiring. So many women will benefit from the stories and lessons she shared.

I also had the pleasure of hiring Heather to speak at the kick-off event for the women's network at our company. She knocked it out of the park! I was amazed at the level of engagement from the group. Additionally, two women applied for senior roles immediately after her session and directly attributed the event in their decision to apply. These were exactly the results we were hoping for!"

—Lisa Propati, vice president
and general manager, Promach

an overachiever's
guide to

breaking

the rules

how to let go of

perfect and

live your truth

heather whelpley

Read Heather's award-winning first book,

An Overachiever's Guide to Breaking the Rules

Let's face it. You've been surrounded by messages your entire life telling you to work harder, produce more, and ALWAYS do your best.

Over time, those messages become rules you follow, often without knowing it. They push you to be productive all the time. They make you believe everything will fall apart if you slow down. They tell you to never disappoint anyone. They make you feel guilty for saying no. They tell you to DO more, WORK more, and BE more.

It's time to stop. It's time to break the rules.

An Overachiever's Guide to Breaking the Rules invites you to get off the hamster wheel, take a breath, and rediscover yourself. This is more than a personal development book. It's an inward journey to free yourself from the weight of perfection and start living your truth.

An Overachiever's Guide to Breaking the Rules has been honored with multiple awards, including the top prize in the motivational category for the Next Generation Indie Book Awards, a Living Now Book Award gold medal in personal growth, short-list for the Grand Prize of the Eric Hoffer Book Award, and a finalist for the First Horizon Book Award.